MANI
His Life and Work
Transforming Evil

I0801365

Mani
(Sketch made from a fragment of wall painting from K'o-cha, China, 8th–9th century)

MANI
His Life and Work
Transforming Evil

Richard Seddon

TEMPLE LODGE

Temple Lodge Publishing
Hillside House, The Square
Forest Row RH18 5ES

www.templelodge.com

Published by Temple Lodge 1998
Second edition 2012

© Richard Seddon 1998

The moral right of the author has been asserted under the Copyright, Designs and Patents Act, 1988

All rights reserved. No part of this publication may be reproduced, stored in a retrieval system, or transmitted, in any form or by any means, electronic, mechanical, photocopying, recording or otherwise, without the prior permission of the publishers

A catalogue record for this book is available from the British Library

ISBN 978 1 906999 33 9

Cover by Andrew Morgan Design, incorporating an illustration of King Bukram-Gur and Mani, 16th century, Tashkent

Typeset by DP Photosetting, Aylesbury, Bucks.
Printed and bound in Great Britain by 4edge Ltd.

Contents

Preface

This study of Manichaeism and of its founder Mani is intended as a general survey of aspects of particular interest to those who have some knowledge of Rudolf Steiner's anthroposophy.

Fragments of Mani's own works and those of his followers are still being found in locations scattered between Egypt and China, and now form a considerable corpus of over ten thousand items. They are first published in specialist journals dealing with the languages concerned. The author is therefore reliant on secondary works that publish selected translations and commentaries in English. The factual information in what follows is taken from one or other of the undermentioned, given in date order, from which original sources can be found if required:

G. Widengren, trans. C. Kessler, *Mani and Manichaeism*, London 1965.

J.P. Asmussen, *Manichaean Literature*, New York 1975.

S.N.C. Lieu, *Manichaeism in the Later Roman Empire and Mediaeval China*, Manchester 1985.

H.-J. Klimkeit, *Gnosis on the Silk Road*, San Francisco 1993.

The latter contains translations of all the main texts from Iranian and Turkish-speaking sources.

Another level of insight, particularly concerning Mani's individuality and his task in the overcoming of evil, has been gained from the spiritual research of Rudolf Steiner. The substance of all his published references to Mani is incorporated, and sources may be found in the Bibliography.

Among other sources particular mention must be made of the work of Albert Steffen and Hugo Reimann. The impetus to study Manichaeism arose from an invitation to speak to the Anthroposophical Schooling Course, for which I am most grateful. Finally, it is a pleasure to acknowledge the help of Margaret Jonas in tracing Steiner's references, and that of George Brown in commenting on the draft; and the tolerance and support of my wife Mary during a stressful time.

Richard Seddon
Advent 1997

Introduction

Evil is nothing new! But we live in an age when evil is more widespread than ever before. One has only to think of words like ethnic cleansing, mafia, paedophilia, drug-dealing, fraud, terrorism—all now commonplace, yet rarely heard even a quarter of a century ago. The media bring such events into every home with startling reality and often relish. They have led vast audiences living humdrum lives to enjoy vicariously such scenes of violence—first at the cinema and on radio, then on television and video—for they know that this is what most of them want. Any thought that fulfilment of such a wish may in turn increase social disturbance is shrugged off as 'unproven'. The whole mood of competition (in education, sport, business, etc.) encourages strife rather than loving help. This harsh culture permeates all the arts, whether popular or modern classical; society at large has become inured to violence. As Steiner put it even in 1906, 'Never yet has mankind passed through a crisis as severe as that of the modern age.'[1] But the symptoms were then mild compared to events today.

At the same time one can only admire the large number of individuals who work with the greatest devotion in the service of others, of the future generation, and of the environment. This is not only in the traditional caring professions, such as medicine and the police, but in many other spheres. It seems as though society is becoming increasingly separated into two groups: the self-seeking and the altruistic.

This situation, particularly in the West, must be seen in the context of two thousand years' work by the Churches and the lawmakers. They have disciplined wrongdoers first by penances or threats of eternal damnation, then by transportation or death, more recently by ever more imprisonment. Today the only ideas are for more police, more prisons, longer sentences and so on. For centuries the religions have supported war, even to impose their own beliefs; sometimes Churches on opposite sides each promised divine support.

But all this is incompatible with the teaching of Christ! For He has said very clearly: 'Do not resist one who is evil. But whoever shall smite thee on thy right cheek, turn to him the other also' (Matt. 5:39). We have been taught to pray for forgiveness 'as we *forgive* them that trespass against us'. And He said to Peter: 'Put up your sword.'

This may at first sight appear to be impractical, though Gandhi recently had considerable success with it. In the long term it is actually the only possible way of overcoming evil, because a person can only transform evil into good within himself, not in someone else. One can of course appeal to the other by preaching or education—as the prison service itself is well aware. But the question is how the other behaves when another opportunity to offend occurs; and it may require some sacrifice to provide that opportunity to consolidate good behaviour.

There are few examples of communities where this Christian principle was fully grasped and applied in practice. One to which Rudolf Steiner repeatedly referred when talking about evil is that founded by Mani in the third century AD, which extended at one time or another from Gaul to China—without ever making use of force.

In the West, Manichaeism was exterminated by the pre-Christian power of the sword at the behest of the Roman Church, and anathematized as a heresy. It is now however recognized as an independent and indeed rival Church or community centred on the impulse of Christ and directed especially to adherents of the great eastern religions, as Mani himself asserted. This was based less on dogma and more on artistic and moral stimulation of the will by means of an imaginative presentation, powerful hymns of praise, and a strict discipline of behaviour and confession of faults. In the East, it was suppressed by the authoritarianism of rulers holding to the decadent pre-Christian religions.

Steiner saw Manichaeism as a spiritual current even more important than Rosicrucianism, although it has as yet received little attention. Its great feature was that it *studied* the role of evil and suffering in the world.[2] What help can it give in the present moral crisis and in the future?

1
Mani's Life and Personality

The founder of Manichaeism was born in Babylonia on 14 April AD 216, and named Kurkabios. Even before his birth, his Parthian father Patik felt called to leave home and join a male community of Jewish Christian Baptists, the Elchasaites. They rejected Paul's writings, and regarded Christ as a great king, reborn many times. So the boy was first brought up by his mother, who was a relative of the (then recently deposed) Parthian royal family and a member of the Christian sect of Marcion.

When he was four his father sent for him to join his community. However, at the age of twelve he received a revelation from a being he called 'the Twin', saying: 'Forsake this congregation! You are not among its followers. The guidance of morals and the restraint of desires are your tasks. Yet because of your youth, the time is not yet come.' Of the Twin he said later: 'I believed him, and that he belongs to me, and that he is a good and useful counsellor. I recognized him, and understood that I am he from whom I was separated. I have borne witness that I myself am he, and am unshaken.' He also said that since his youth he came under special divine protection and instruction—Angels and powers of holiness brought him up through visions and signs.

What happened then is unclear. It was previously thought that he went to Baghdad and studied the eastern religious literatures available there, but a more recently found text suggests that he waited. Further confusion is caused by an alternative story fabricated by Church opponents and referred to by Rudolf Steiner.[1] Briefly, this tells of a merchant named Skythianos, his wife educated in Egypt, and a pupil Terebinthos. The latter escaped to Persia with four books by Skythianos, which he left on his death to a widow with whom he lodged. She in turn died, leaving them to her twelve-year-old slave boy named Corbicius, who published them as his own under the name of Mani. Though now known to be untrue, this points to connections with Skythianos, actually the great initiate of western occultism about the time of Christ, and with Egypt.

Whatever happened, he must have come across many differing religious sects:

- The Christian followers of Marcion (d. 160) – such as his mother – who rejected the Old Testament, and regarded Jehovah as vain, unethical and war-loving, but revered the God of the New Testament, because He sent His only Son to redeem mankind (as described by Paul and in their version of Luke, which was expurgated of the genealogy, nativity, baptism and temptation).
- Followers of Bardaisan (154–222), philosopher, astrologer and man of the world, who held the controversial view that darkness was no mere absence of light but an active, invading and contaminating force. Man lived amidst the four elements, with free will to choose between the divine and the darkness. Through Christ came resurrection of souls, but not of bodies.
- A profusion of differing Gnostic schools, which spoke of salvation through revelation, and of esoteric knowledge from the ancient Mysteries; of a transcendent God wholly good and unknowable, and an imperfect world of matter and evil, the product of a fallen emanation, the Demiurge; of man's fleshly nature as the product of desire, yet his soul containing seeds of the divine planted by the spirit or mind (Nous) but unaware of it; of Christ as divine but never truly man, who only appeared to suffer; of salvation through awakening to the call from above.
- In addition there were the prevailing Zoroastrianism and

its modified form of Zurvanism; Buddhism from India; Hermeticism from Egypt; and various Jewish sects.
- Above all, it was usual among the Parthian upper classes to which he belonged to be initiated into the Mysteries of Mithra (see Appendix 1).

Out of all this, the growing youth found his own way. He himself said that he recognized the revelations of Seth, Enosh, Enoch and Shem; Buddha, Zoroaster and Jesus; Paul and Nikotheos (who wrote of man as 'phos'—light—and of light-particles redeemed by Jesus).

At the age of 24, Mani received a second inspiration from the Twin saying: 'You are not sent only to this sect, but to every people and school of learning; for this hope will be made manifest and preached by you in every clime and zone of the world. Go from here and travel about. For I will be with you as your helper and protector wherever you preach what I have revealed. Therefore do not grieve and feel depressed.' A Coptic text adds:

> He revealed to me the hidden Mystery, hidden from the ages and generations of men, the mystery of the depths and the heights, the mystery of light and darkness, the mystery of the contest, the war, and the great battle caused by darkness. He revealed to me how light and darkness together gave rise to the world ... the creation of Adam ... the mystery of the Tree of Knowledge of which Adam ate, by which his eyes were made to see, the mystery of the Apostles sent out to select the churches. Thus did the Paraclete disclose to me all that has been and all that will be, and all that the eye sees and the ear hears and the thought thinks. Through Him I learned to know everything, I saw the All through Him, and I became one body and one spirit (with Him).

It was only at this point that Kurkabios took the name 'Mani'. It means Manas-bearer, or bearer of the spirit-self which can say 'I am the I am'.[2] The form 'Manes' is now rarely used.

After converting his family, Mani sailed to India, probably to Turan, the ancient enemy of Iran, where Buddhism was strong. In Zarathustrian tradition it was also the site of the future Paradise. A year later he returned to the Babylon area and converted the newly crowned ruler.

> By his miraculous power he showed the Paradise of Light with all the gods, divine Beings, and the immortal breath of life, a garden with all kinds of things, and also other splendid things there. Thereafter (the ruler) fell to the ground unconscious for three hours, and what he saw he kept in his heart. Then the Apostle put his hand upon his head and he regained consciousness. When he had risen, he fell down at the Apostle's feet and seized his right hand...

This ruler was a brother of the Sasanian Great King Shapur I, 'worshipper of Ahura Mazda, King of Kings of Iran and non-Iran, of the race of the gods' according to an inscription. Mani thus gained access, and when Shapur saw light emanating from Mani's shoulder he was welcomed, given letters of protection, and allowed to preach his religion throughout the empire, despite protest from the established Zoroastrian priesthood. He is said to have become a royal retainer for some time, and to have 'fought at the king's side' in the West. Supported by disciples, he extended his work both westwards to Egypt and eastwards to Khorasan, his Parthian homeland, where he addressed in particular kings, queens and the nobility. Syrian authors say he spent much time in India, Kashmir, Turkestan, Tibet and China, but met much resistance. Little more is known of him until his last days, but a fine imaginative reconstruction has been dramatized by Albert Steffen (see Appendix 2).

What we do know is that he was no abstract theologian or philosopher, but an initiate who founded his own religion on the basis of his revelation, and felt free to adopt or fiercely reject the dogmas of religions around him. With the natural authority due to his royal descent and a vivid sense of mission, he had the strength of mind to develop from a lone preacher to the organizer of a widespread community, while expounding its spiritual foundations and establishing its rituals.

It is significant that he is still known in Islam not as a religious leader but as an artist. He is said to have withdrawn for a year to a cave, emerging with pictures on a scroll of extraordinary beauty, 'the likeness of that which he created out of his mind'. He also created frescoes and miniatures, and developed the crafts of calligraphy and book-production. He loved music, ascribing to it a divine origin; he composed hymns and songs, encouraged singing, and is said to have created a new style of string music. Yet his most lasting art was that of a writer: 'For the Apostles my brothers who came before me did not write down their wisdom as I wrote mine, nor painted their wisdom in pictures like mine.' 'Let him who hears these truths in words also see them in an image, and let him who is unable to learn them from words learn them from pictures'. He encouraged translations of his works: 'They give the revelation and wisdom in different forms, for the languages to which they are sent are not the same.'

His own writings (mainly in Aramaic/Syrian, not Babylonian) include: The Living Gospel (fragments), The Treasures of Life (extracts in Augustine), Treatise (lost), Book of Mysteries (lost), and a Book of Giants (with the fall of Angels from Genesis 6, the book of Enoch, and a legend of the giant Ogia who after the flood fought a dragon); cosmological and eschatological writings in Middle Persian addressed to Shapur; Homilies (including a life of Buddha/ Barlaam and Joasaph, folklore, and fables such as Aesop); Prayers and Confessions, and one of the largest and oldest collections of Hymns and Psalms (lost in the last war); letters (mainly lost); biographical fragments; and a picture book (lost).

> In his unpretentious, simple sermons he used all the similies and allegories of Gnostic language, becoming particularly graphic through his numerous illustrations, tragic, comic, even coarse, taken from fables, horror stories and everyday life. Without pedantry, he had great vivacity to capture his audience ... His hymns and psalms richly deployed sacred poetry ... His dogmatic texts have the balance of architectural masterpieces, which aided committal to memory.[3]

If a Chinese text is to be believed:

> He had great powers of concentration, and understood the Way ... His bodily condition was exceptionally fine. His perception embraced heaven and earth, and his knowledge penetrated the sun and moon ... He put an end to muddiness and extolled clarity. His words were simple, his reasoning straight, his actions correct and his testimonies true.

He was most interested in cosmological ideas, though he gives no explanations of such things as solstices, eclipses or phases of the moon. He also practised as a healer: 'May the spirit of fever called Idra come out in the name of Lord Jesus the Friend, of His Father the Highest, and of the Holy Spirit ... of Michael, Raphael and Gabriel ...'

Mani introduced himself in his Gospel and in letters as 'I, Mani, apostle of Jesus Christ'. His aim was to make Christ accessible to adherents of every faith, thus harmonizing and revitalizing previous religions, not obliterating them (a parable compares his religion with the great ocean, into which all rivers flow). For this, the presentation of his central doctrine in the form of an imaginative drama (Chapter 2) was especially apt. However, his emphasis as a Christian on individual freedom was incompatible with King Shapur's demand for submission to the state. Tension developed, and he was blamed for failing to heal Shapur's eldest son.

After Shapur's death the young King Hormisdar renewed Mani's safe conduct, but he died after two years. His brother Barham, however, followed the Zurvan priesthood at a time of nationalistic renewal (in so far as he had any interest other than hunting!). He was also jealous that Mani had revelations, while he, the Great King, did not. Mani was therefore recalled, impeached as a traitor by the Magi, imprisoned, tortured, and died after 26 days at the age of 60 in AD 277.

His body was cut up, the head displayed above the gate of Gundeshapur, and the remains buried by his adherents at Ctesiphon. But 'in great joy he flew, together with light-gods going to right and left of him, with harp sound and song of joy, in divine miraculous power, like a swift lightning and shooting star, to the column of glory, the path of light, and the moon-chariot, meeting place with the gods'. His death was called by his followers 'the Passion or Crucifixion of the Illuminator', and was regarded as a Mystery experience, though distorted to mockery. His last prayer is reported in Appendix 3.

Twelve thousand Manichaeans were executed in the three years of Barham's rule, and this continued under his successor.

2
The Cosmic Drama[1]

Before heaven and earth existed, the unbegotten Father of Greatness, breathing the unbegotten air (ether) of the unbegotten realm, sat enthroned and wreathed in flowers. His fourfold majesty consisted of light, power and wisdom embraced within a single divinity; and his limbs or dwellings comprised reason, mind, intelligence, thought and understanding. With him were the Aeons, his twelve sons, and manifold Aeons of the Aeons, as well as his consort or twin, the Great Spirit, whose breath fed them with its light and life. Everything was peace and harmony, in a mood of pure contemplation.

On three sides this kingdom of light was unbounded, but southwards and downwards there was a wedge of darkness like a smoky lunar landscape. There, while its inhabitants were jostling and chasing one another in passion and blind frenzy, the swirling agitation once carried them to the border with the realm of light. They caught a glimpse of that realm, and became seized with longing for it. So they ceased their strife, to consider how they could mingle with the good they had seen, armed for attack, and demons of all kinds burst in.

The Father of Light had consequently to step from repose and contemplation to action. They were to be stopped, but there was in his kingdom only goodness, so that punishment could not be considered. He accordingly sent forth from himself the Mother of Life, who amidst great rejoicing called forth Primal Man. He armed himself with the five pure elements of the kingdom of light—ether, wind, light, water and fire—as his living soul or self, and descended into darkness. But he had to accept defeat. He was robbed of his armour, which the demons of darkness devoured. But being of an essentially different nature, it crept into their inmost parts and acted as a deadly poison, bringing death into their kingdom. Their desire to invade was assuaged, yet thereafter particles of light were dispersed everywhere throughout the darkness.

Primal Man lay in the abyss of matter, stunned, fettered, and surrounded by wild beasts and demons. But his divine intelligence reminded him of his origin, and in response to his sevenfold prayer to the Mother of Life, and her entreaty to the Father of Light, the latter called forth the Friend of Light, who evoked the Great Builder. From him issued the Living Spirit, who with his five sons went to the border of darkness and uttered a Call to Primal Man: Peace be upon you, excellent one amid the evil ones, lustrous one amid darkness! Primal Man heard and responded: Come with peace, bringing goods of rest and peace! This Answer ascended to the Living Spirit, who extended his right hand, and this was seized by Primal Man. He was drawn up, soaring back with the Mother of Life to the Paradise of Light amidst much joy.

Nevertheless the five elements, his proper soul, were still fettered and defiled within the darkness. To liberate them, the Living Spirit flayed the demonic princes of darkness, chaining the five classes of demons to the five elements. Then, while his son the Holder of Glory held high the ten heavens, he formed the sky from their skins, the mountains from their bones, and the earth from their fragments. And while another son Atlas held on his shoulders the eight layers of earth, he created the sun and moon from uncontaminated particles of light, and the stars from those only lightly sullied.

To recover the light from the corrupt mass remaining, the Father of Light now evoked the Third Messenger. The latter then set the world in motion through days and nights and seasons; and he created a Column of Glory, three cosmic wheels of wind, water and fire, which drew up particles of light so that in the first half of each month they filled the moon, and in the second half were conducted to the sun, and thence to the New Paradise of Light. He then evoked the twelvefold Maiden of Light. She sailed across heaven in the moon, by the radiant naked beauty of her femininity stimulating the male demons to discharge as sperm particles which fell to earth accompanied by sin, and gave rise to five kinds of trees and plants. He himself sailed across heaven in the sun, by his shining naked youth stimulating the female demons to give premature birth to five kinds of animals, which devoured the light in the fruits of the trees. The sin that had fallen into water was slain by another son of the Living Spirit, the Adamas of Light.

In a desperate attempt to preserve the remaining light, matter—in the person of Az, greed and lust—plotted to concentrate it and pass it on through continual reproduction. A male archon of darkness engulfed all the male demons and monsters, and a female archon engulfed all the females. Through their union were created Adam and Eve, but they were shaped through the presence of the Third Messenger and Maiden of Light above them. They were thus a microcosmic mixture of light and darkness, blind, deaf, and unaware either of the light within them or of the greed, lust, envy and hate impressed into their bodies.

Texts differ as to who took the initiative to free Adam, but to do so the Third Messenger sent to him Jesus the Splendour. He woke Adam, took hold of him and stirred him to life, exorcised and fettered the demons, showed him the Father in the heights and his own self, raised him and made him eat of the Tree of Life, and instructed him in the gnosis of what was, what is, and what will be.

Jesus warned Adam against intercourse with Eve, and he overcame greed and lust by continence. But the male archon had intercourse with her, and she bore Cain, and by him Abel. Both had daughters through her and intermarried. A demon then gave Abel's wife two children, for which Abel blamed Cain in front of Eve, infuriating Cain, who killed him. The demon then taught Eve to entice Adam, and they had Seth. Again the demon enticed Eve to ensnare Adam, but Seth persuaded him to go east to the Light and Wisdom of God. Adam could thus enter the kingdom of light after death, but Eve and her offspring could not.

3
Stages of Evolution

By casting his central message not in earthly laws like the stone tablets of Moses but in this great cosmic imagination, Mani made it accessible to the peoples of the East, who could grasp it with the atavistic but nevertheless spiritual capacities of the sentient soul, or echoes of yet earlier stages. It thus opened a means for the impulse of Christ to transform these beliefs, in such a way that the Egypto-Chaldean wisdom might become fruitful for the fifth post-Atlantean age, the Persian for the sixth, and the Indian for the seventh age. The form of Christianity suited to the burgeoning intellectual soul of the West, where Plotinus was already carrying thinking to the abstract heights of Neoplatonism, was unable to achieve such transformations.

The drama echoes a widely-known story about the descent of the soul to acquire the 'pearl' of the ego, while there underlies its formulation a picture of the evolution of the world and mankind that was taught in the ancient Mysteries. This was first presented in a form suited to modern consciousness by Rudolf Steiner in his book *Occult Science – An Outline*. For Mani too this was an absolutely real process, at once both material and spiritual.

The drama opens in the realm of the Father of Greatness or of Light, whose characteristic is 'dominion' or holding sway. The unbegotten realm was equated by Mani's followers with the Milky Way. Augustine reported that it and its air/ether were of one substance with the Father. This accords with Zarathustra's primal reality of Being, the god Zurvan or Zervane Akarene, the realm of calm undifferentiated duration, not yet isolated into individual moments[1] and regarded as beyond reach on any inner or outer path of knowledge.[2] The mood is one of pure contemplation (the gnostic conception of the Father) and of silence.[3] His twelve sons, each with their twelve Aeons, express the powers directed from cosmic depths towards the zodiac, intrinsically neither good nor evil (see Chapter 5).

Only when we come to concepts of motion (e.g. chasing), the spiritual reality from which concepts of time and space derive, does darkness manifest. (Accusations in Catholic and Turkish sources that Mani regarded evil as of *equal* origin with God are therefore inaccurate, though he undoubtedly regarded them as originally *separate*.) Darkness is primarily a realm of activity, of will. This corresponds to Steiner's description of the Saturn stage of evolution, where the Spirits of Will first pour into the field of the zodiac their activity that is, like all willing, dark (i.e. outside the light of consciousness). The result is the creation of Time Spirits as ego-beings; and entry into time brings the possibility to progress faster (as Archai) or remain behind (as Asuras), and hence the possibility of evil (see Chapter 5).

Within this darkness then arise rage and longing (Lucifer or Az) and plans to attack by force (Ahriman or Simnu). Recognition of two distinct sources of sin and evil respectively recur in Mani's work. He said, for example: 'Even now the Holy Spirit accompanies me, keeps and protects me. And in its power I fight Az and Ahriman. And I teach men wisdom and knowledge, and save them from Az and Ahriman.' He may have learned of the 'middle way' from either Mithraism or Buddhism (moderation in all things). He certainly saw the significance of the crucifixion of Christ between two thieves, one of whom repented and could be redeemed. This is fundamental to an understanding of Manichaeism, as of Christianity itself, which western culture has still to learn.

Equally fundamental is that the Father of Greatness could not punish, because he had only goodness at his disposal. A late Manichaean text personalizes this by saying: 'Whoever strikes you, do not strike him again. And whoever hates you, do not hate him back. And whoever envies you, do not envy him in turn. And whoever is angry with you, always speak with kindness to him. And what you detest in another, do not do yourself. No, one has to endure insults and other abuses, they shall not in any way be able to make the devout one waver ...' This is the true Christian path of mildness or meekness in practical life: 'Blessed are the meek, for they shall inherit the earth' (Matt. 5:5).

* * *

The second stage begins when the Father of Light sends forth from himself the soul-force called the Mother of Life, who personifies 'wisdom'. This corresponds to the sacrifice of their substance by the Spirits of Wisdom at the Sun stage of evolution. They give rise to the life-body or etheric body, and thus to the archetype or thought-form of mankind called Primal Man or—in Chinese texts—First Thought. He represents 'Victory or Salvation'. The macrocosmic creative forces of the zodiac were researched in the Mythraic (inner) Mysteries,[4] and were known in Hebrew tradition as Adam Kadmon and in the Scandinavian Edda as Ymir. They were guided by the Spirits of Wisdom to create the human organization under the leadership of the Regent of the Sun evolution, known to us as Christ and to Zarathustrian tradition as Ahura Mazda or Ormuzd, whom Mani equated with Primal Man. In Zarathustrian teaching Ahura Mazda and Ahriman were twin sons of Zurvan, Ahriman as the untransformed darkness of Saturn being the firstborn (but Mani did *not* adopt this).

Thus Primal Man, as spirit, descends with his five sons, the five elements in etheric form, said to represent 'contentment'. Since he follows the divine principle of mildness, his defeat is inevitable—but this is what enables evolution to progress. Augustine complained that in the Manichaean view 'the good and true God, through Primal Man, mingled a part of himself with the prince of darkness, which part is defiled the world over'. But without the presence of light in matter, matter could not be redeemed. New emanations are called forth for this purpose: first the Friend of Light, who represents 'zeal, diligence'; from him comes the Great Builder, representing 'truth'; and thirdly the Living Spirit, the personification of 'faith' who also has five sons (Chapter 6).

The Living Spirit (identified in Persia with Mithra) is the second to approach the darkness, but does not at first penetrate it. The dramatic ritual of battle, defeat, awakening, dialogue and salvation had already been prefigured in the rescue of Tammuz by Ishtar in Chaldean tradition. Now, however, it is presented as a rhythmic process between above and below, with the addition of the call, response, extended hand and ascent; and rhythm is characteristic of the Sun evolution. Call and Response are portrayed by Mani as themselves spiritual beings, the sixth sons of the Living Spirit and Primal Man respectively, together comprising the Thought of Life. Whenever a soul prays for redemption the Call is said to recur, and if it is heard and the Response made, then the hand of salvation is always extended. From this offering of the right hand grew the Manichaean greeting with the right hand, as a symbol of salvation from the darkness.

* * *

With the devouring, by the demons of darkness, of the light brought by Primal Man, we reach the Moon stage of evolution, and also one of the most important conceptions of Manichaeism. It means that henceforth there is no element of darkness that does not have within it a greater or lesser degree of light. Or, to put it differently, nowhere does matter exist without spirit. There is no cleft between them; nothing is without a moral aspect. For the light brought by Primal Man as his 'living soul' is not the everyday light whose effects are sense-perceptible, but the substance of the Father of Light. This unmanifest light is the first supersensible element experienced by spiritual vision, an inner experience much more powerful and inwardly alive than thinking.[5] And Mani and his Elect still, of course, had the clairvoyance to see this. It is the fundamental essence of all existence (the 'thing in itself' which Kant declared unknowable) out of which matter condenses into existence. Spiritual science asserts: 'Every substance upon earth is condensed light.'[6] For Manichaeans this light was the divine element imprisoned in every plant, animal, human, and even the earth; and it must be redeemed.

We normally grasp only a shadow of this reality as the concept. As such it brings form, rigidity and, therefore, death into the whirling chaos. Even the particles of modern physics are no more than such thought-constructs. Scholasticism, however, distinguished the three aspects: the creative spiritual reality, such as the species (*universalia ante rem*); the essence of the natural object, where its interweaving with darkness (both in themselves supersensible) gives the sense-experience of colour, etc. (*universalia in re*); and the reflection in our thinking (*universalia post rem*).

Augustine rightly said that the Manichaeans 'consider all souls, not only of men but even of beasts, to be of the substance of God and altogether parts of God'. Mani's description of the five elements as the soul or self of Primal Man points to the sacrifice of the substance of the astral body by the Spirits of Motion during the Moon stage of evolution. It was during Moon evolution that the fluid and chemical processes forming the essence of digestion first arose, enabling the demons to 'devour' the light particles. During Moon evolution too the moon and earth were first separated from the sun by the Spirits of Motion; and this is depicted by the separation out of the firmament and the formation of the sun and moon by the Living Spirit and his five sons (who represent planetary forces—see Chapter 6).

As Mani said, 'the universe created was to become a hospital for light and a prison for darkness'.

* * *

With the advent of the Third Messenger (representing 'purity') we reach Earth evolution as we know it, and the destiny of mankind. He sets going afresh what comes over from previous stages, and with his twelvefold emanation the Maiden of Light ('harmony, mildness') brings into being the plants and animals of the physical sense-perceptible world. This corresponds to the formative activity of the Spirits of Form. Their sacrifice of the substance of the human ego is depicted in the Column of Glory ('righteousness') which provides a path for the light within man to rise through the cosmos to the New Paradise. But through the intervention of Az (Lucifer), who takes hold of the hitherto innocent sexual polarity, Adam and Eve are brought into existence—neither as divine beings nor as the crown of the animal kingdom, but as pitiful remnants torn off by the demons from the soul of Primal Man, overwhelmed by darkness.

> Into the body of Adam Az sowed desire and lust, covetousness and the urge to mate, enmity and slander, envy and sinfulness, wrath and impurity, darkening of the mind and unconsciousness, hostility to religion and doubt, to steal and lie, to rob and do evil deeds, obstinacy and falsehood, vengefulness and conceit, anxiety and grief, sorrow and pain, poverty and want, illness and infirmity of old age, offensiveness and thievishness. And she gave to her creatures as many languages and tongues as the issue of the monster demons had . . .

So deeply did the Manichaeans experience the Fall.

4
Redemption

The drama reaches a climax in the redemption of Adam from his unconsciousness by the sending of Jesus the Splendour, which stands as an archetype for the subsequent redemption of each individual through Christ. In eastern texts the initiative to send him starts with the Third Messenger, a non-committal name which adherents of other religions can interpret in their own tradition as Mithra, Maitreya or whoever. The East did not have the same longing as the West to identify a specific physical person as Messiah.

In Manichaean texts there are three different images of Jesus, which were not always clearly distinguished:

- Jesus the Messiah was the historical manifestation described in the Gospels. The Manichaeans said clearly of him: Mariam's son cannot be the son of God: a god does not feel himself betrayed and deserted, a god is not crucified by his father.
- Jesus the Splendour, the Jesus of Light, or Brilliant Jesus was the inwardly experienced Being who brought gnosis and hence redemption to mankind. He was wholly divine, the supreme revealer and guide, of whom Mani was the Apostle. He was first made manifest at the Baptism in Jordan. This is emphasized in various anathemas, especially the 'Seven Chapters' from Mount Athos, where he is also said to have been identified with the sun.[1] However, from his Gnostic upbringing, Mani held that 'the light shone in the darkness, but the darkness received it not'. But he could not take the further step of John: 'the Logos became flesh and dwelt among us'. Rather 'it did not touch the flesh, so that it was not

overpowered, nor made capable of suffering and transient. How should it suffer, since the darkness neither had power over it nor darkened its effectiveness?' As Steiner put it: 'Mani perceived Christ in heavenly glory, as one who lived in a phantom body, an etheric body, upon earth, but he could not see how he took up his abode in human flesh.'[2] The suffering, death and resurrection were not the real experiences of this Being, but only an appearance. The Great Nous or Cosmic Intelligence, the inspirer of all religions, he saw as an emanation of this Jesus.

- The Suffering Jesus shared in the real and universal suffering of the element of light, including that in every stone and plant (especially in trees, which formed the Cross). This is the Jesus who will remain with us until the end of the earth, when he will appear as Jesus the Judge. The slow salvation of mankind is at the same time His own redemption. This corresponds to Steiner's view of Christ as Spirit of the Earth. He was affirmed in a Coptic hymn:

> The strangers with whom I mixed, Me they knew not.
> They tasted My sweetness, they desired to keep Me with them,
> I am life to them, but they were death to Me.
> I bore up beneath them, they wore Me as a garment upon them.
> I am in everything, I bear the skies, I am the foundation,
> I support the earths, I am the light that shines forth, that gives joy to souls.
> I am the life of the world, I am the milk that is in all trees.
> I am the sweet water that is beneath the sons of matter.[3]

In contrast, of Jesus the Splendour:

I am the redeeming god, and the root and ground of your soul,
Who are born from me and made visible from the beginning of life till now.
You are the garment of my body,
And I am your heart, and the strength of your limbs.
You are my ... I have fought with you the demons and rulers of hell.
... You are the substance of the whole building
And I am your splendour ... the lord of your beauty.
Through you I made visible the battle against every sign
And you yourself did become light in great strength.
I am your strength and your ... mind.

* * *

The 'exorcizing and fettering of demons' is the purification of the inner life. Mani said elsewhere: 'I was seized by numberless disgusting demons, who made me their prisoner. They subjugated me, tore me to pieces and ate me. Demons, imps and witches, dark dragons, ugly, stinking and black—from them I had much pain and death. All cry out upon me and attack, pursue, rise against me.' We live in an age that derides such concepts, hiding them under the carpet of psychological terminology. But that does not mean that they are not still here; it simply enables them to be more active without being observed and opposed.

In showing Adam his Father in the heights and his own self—that he is formed out of the archetype of Primal Man brought again by the Third Messenger, but is only a pitiful remnant of what he might have been and must become—there is wrung from him the tragic lament: 'Woe, woe to the maker of my body, and to the one who has held my soul in bondage, and the rebels who have enslaved me.' The image of Paradise is shrunk and shrivelled due to the activities of Lucifer and Ahriman.[4] This is expressed in various forms:

- To you I will sing, skilled god, living soul, gift from the Father ... I am a god, born of gods, brilliant, flashing and bright, shining, fragrant and lovely. But I have come into misery.
- The true self comes from the transcendent world of light, and remains united with it. The only way to salvation is to know this. To know oneself is to recover this true self which has fallen, by means of the Nous.
- Teach that pious and sinful thoughts are intermixed, and separate the one from the other. Understand your being, and the pure Word that is master of the soul in the body. Through it learn to see through the false word that leads to the hell of darkness. Remember the rebirths ...

The raising of Adam points to the significance of the vertical human posture, in contradistinction to the animal, which makes possible the entry of the ego that can relate equally to heaven and earth.

Since the Tree of Knowledge was eaten, the Tree of Life had been forbidden mankind. But Mani must have realized that one day it must again be eaten, for 'I am the way, the truth *and* the life'.

Finally Adam received the gnosis of what was, what is, and what will be. The previous chapter concerned 'what was'. The most important aspect of Manichaeism is its general attitude towards 'what is', namely, that no cleft divides the spiritual from the material world (p. 20). 'Manichaeans spoke of the spiritual facts in the stars and their courses, in the mystery of the sun, in the same way as they spoke of moral phenomena or happenings in human evolution. Hence their concepts were not abstract, cut off from reality, but real conceptions that had sufficient force to play a part in outer nature. Their whole content was the conquest of evil, of matter, by thought.'[5]

As regards 'what is to be', though broad outlines were foreseen in the Mysteries, hardly any trace had entered the religions beyond the promise of a forthcoming Messiah. Only through Christ came the strength for the uninitiated to receive without harm a knowledge of the future, beginning with Mark 13 and extended by Paul to the successive appearance, revelation and coming again of Christ. It was John who first wrote down for the priesthood in his Apocalypse a living and ongoing picture of what is to come, setting goals for human wills. The fragments of Mani's presentation will be considered in Chapter 11.

The epilogue concerning Eve's offspring, only briefly outlined above, is clearly a forerunner of the first part of the Temple Legend used in Freemasonry, but the details and hence the moral implications are quite different.[6] It serves here to emphasize the ever-present role of darkness in human life, the reality of the 'Double', and the need to resist its lures. Seth and the priestly line stand as a model of 'religious behaviour', whereas the significance and destiny of Cain and his successors is left open.

5
Twelve Realms of Light

Augustine held that human beings are predestined to be either good or evil, and that the good must destroy the evil. For the Manichaeans, however, evil is an integral part of the cosmos, collaborating in its evolution, finally to be transformed and transfigured, not destroyed, by the good.[1]

A text from Turfan gives an exoteric indication of the way the Manichaeans worked rhythmically with good and evil forces over a period of three days, against the background of their myth:

> The first day is the Light-Nous. Its twelve hours are the twelve great kings of triumphant mien. They are: the Great King, wisdom, victory, joy, application to life, truth, faith, enduring insult, sincerity, good action, impartiality, complete inner and outer light.
>
> The first night is the demon of desires. Its twelve hours are bones, muscles, veins, flesh, skin combined with hatred, obduracy, instinctiveness, impatience, stupidity as well as the flames of lusts and sensory desires.
>
> The second day is the pure life-principle of the New Man. Its twelve hours are the twelve brilliant kings of the second transformation.
>
> The second night is the violently burning and poisonous flames of sensory desires. Its twelve hours are the twelve dark and poisoned thoughts. This night symbolizes the first result of the demons.
>
> On the third day are the 'call' and the 'harkening'. Its twelve hours are Nous, mind, intelligence, thought and understanding combined with love, faith, perfecting, perseverance and wisdom.
>
> Through this gradually ripen an endless profusion of fruits which manifest in the community of adepts.[2]

Because of successive translations including Chinese, these terms can only approximate to the originals. We may note the clear distinction between the demons of desire (i.e. Az, Lucifer) who are concerned with aspects of body and soul, and the dark and poisoned thoughts of Ahriman, that must be countered in spirit.

An outstanding aspect is that both good and evil are characterized in terms of twelve 'hours', the twelvefoldness of the cosmos. That Mani connected human destiny with the zodiac in this way was an echo of the clairvoyance of the Egypto-Chaldean age.[3] Rudolf Steiner described the connection by saying:

> What is symbolized by the twelve sons, the twelve points of the zodiac, is more sublime than the earthly opposition between good and evil. In the astral realm something which from one point of view works for good may from another point of view appear as evil. That which is the symbol of the Gods in the twelve points of space—which are permanent throughout the process of evolution through Saturn, Sun, Moon and Earth—is above good and evil. But the evolving of the earth in the course of time can only happen by a division in the permanent deities into a sphere of good and a sphere of evil. In themselves none are either good or evil, but in their influence upon the earth each is sometimes good, sometimes evil. Of the twelve points of permanence, five remain within the sphere of good, and two on the border, making seven. Hence comes the conception that seven signs of the zodiac belong to the world of light, to the upper world, and that the lower five, beginning with Scorpion, belong to the world of darkness.[4]

Evil is in fact nothing but good that is ill-timed, nothing else than the divine. When life that is formless meets resistance, as in a plant, it is hardened into form. Similarly 'when what is good strives to be preserved it becomes rigid, it becomes evil. This interweaving of good and evil is a gradual process. If what is good is to remain good, it must constantly harmonize with what hinders it—such is the Manichaean teaching.[5]

Thus 'if we ever find a place where specially evil beings exist, we can be very sure that with them are connected other higher beings who have so great a power for what is good, beautiful and sublime that they are able to guide even the lowest forces back to what is good. Evil and ugliness need to exist, because without them human beings could never become independent through choosing in freedom between them and goodness.'[6]

The twelve 'hours' of the first day quoted above in fact refer to the principal beings of the cosmic drama, as follows:

Turfan Text	*Character*	*Predicate of Character*
Great King	Father of Light	Dominion
Wisdom	Mother of Life	Wisdom
Victory	Primal Man	Victory, Salvation
Joy	His Five Sons	Contentment, Joy
Application to Life	Friend of Light	Zeal, Diligence
Truth	Great Builder	Truth
Faith	Living Spirit	Faith
Enduring Insult	Third Messenger	Patience
Sincerity	Column of Glory	Righteousness
Good Action	Jesus the Splendour	Kindness
Impartiality	Maiden of Light	Harmony, Mildness
Inner and Outer Light	Great Nous	Light from World of Light

The question must now arise, how these twelve 'hours' or characters relate to the constellations; and the same must be asked of the twelve hours of the first night. It has not yet proved possible to resolve these questions. But if we take as the 'twelve dark and poisoned thoughts' of the second night the twelve 'evil thoughts which proceed from within out of the heart of man and defile the man' enumerated by Christ (Mark 7:21), then this can be done; for they correlate with twelve Virtues related by H.P. Blavatsky to the zodiac, confirmed and extended by Rudolf Steiner (see Appendix 4) as follows:[7]

Zodiac	*Blavatsky*		*Steiner*	*Evil*
Virgin	Courtesy	becomes	Tact of Heart	Fornications
Lion	Compassion	"	Freedom	Thefts
Crab	Selflessness	"	Catharsis	Murders
Twins	Perseverance	"	Faithfulness	Adulteries
Bull	Balance	"	Progress	Covetousness
Ram	Devotion	"	Force of Sacrifice	Malice
Fishes	Magnanimity	"	Love	Deceit
Waterman	Discretion	"	Meditative Force	Indecency
Goat	Courage	"	Redemptive Force	Envy
Archer	Control of Tongue	"	Feeling for Truth	Slander
Scorpion	Patience	"	Insight	Arrogance
Scales	Contentment	"	Equanimity	Folly

We can gain some confidence in this correlation through the connection between the zodiac and successive cultural ages.[8] Looking first at the pre-Christian ages of the post-Atlantean period, we can compare the foregoing with the Ten Commandments of Moses (Deut. 5) as follows:

Culture	*Zodiac*	*Evil*	*Commandments*	
Indian	Crab	Murders	v. 17	Thou shalt do no murder
Persian	Twins	Adulteries	v. 18	Neither shalt thou commit adultery
Egypto-Chaldean	Bull	Covetousness	v. 19	Neither shalt thou steal
Graeco-Roman	Ram	Malice	v. 20	Neither shalt thou bear false witness

If we now look at the ages after the turning-point of the coming of Christ and the entry into the five evil constellations between Scorpion and Fishes, we find:

Culture	*Zodiac*	*Evil*	*Virtue*
Present	Fishes	Deceit	Magnanimity becomes Love
Sixth (Russian)	Waterman	Indecency	Discretion becomes Meditative Force
Seventh	Goat	Envy	Courage becomes Redemptive Force

It is not difficult to recognize deceit as characteristic of modern life today, in its many forms of lies, fraud, duplicity, lack of openness (hiding one's faults) and so on; above all the whole deceit of materialism when extended beyond the mineral kingdom leads us even to doubt our own thoughts about the spirit. In all this Ahriman first becomes predominant.

Moreover the residual forces of the earlier cultures, now out of their due time, work on as hardened relics that oppose progressive evolution to a culture of initiation knowledge, and bring about social chaos. Buddha indeed taught that desire (i.e. covetousness) was the beginning of all suffering. In the process of establishing the reality of our ego, we frequently exude malice, hatred of the spirit in the other person, to the extent that we live amidst a kind of War of All Against All. And our society's covetousness for the comforts of the sense world frightens us off from venturing to be as spiritually creative as we could. We are not always fully conscious of all this, but enter into it at night—and then it is reflected back to us from the earth in the darkness of our instincts, impulses, desires and passions. As Mani puts it, the light is devoured by the beings of darkness. In contrast, we can understand that the special virtue of the present age is that 'magnanimity (open-heartedness) becomes love'.

We can also sense a foretaste of the sixth age, when indecency, pandering to the lower sexual instincts, undermines the discretion necessary for development of meditative force, which even now should be preparing the way for a fully conscious reception of the spirit-self (Manas) in a broad spectrum of mankind. In Steiner's words:

> Today evil tendencies are present subconsciously in every human being—there is not a crime to which everyone of today is not subconsciously prone (though whether this leads to an evil action depends on quite different circumstances). The purpose of these forces, before they are perverted by the social order, is ... to enable people to break through to the life of the spirit at the level of the consciousness soul. Evil actions are only a caricature. One important impulse in this age is to develop active concern for one's neighbour ... A deep inner experience of art enables one to perceive the spiritual archetype of another person through his visible picture-nature—the

> form of his head, his gait ... We must no longer see him as a combination of bones, muscles, blood and so on, but as the image of his eternal spiritual being.[9]

The Acts of John (27:9), an apocryphal book regarded as Manichaean, makes very clear this need to penetrate beyond the person visible to the senses to the real human being.

6
Fivefold Aspects

It was probably from his connection with Mithraism that Mani heard of the soul's descent through the five planetary spheres, the forces of which were there regarded as manifestations of vices, whereas sun and moon were regarded as good. But Mani also recognized the positive aspects of the planetary spheres, which he described from three aspects. For Mani wrote, like Paul, of the threefold nature of man: body (*soma, tan*); soul (*psyche, menog*) and spirit (*pneuma, gyan*):

> From that which I have written above, it is clear to the discerning that the spirit of the body [i.e. etheric] is of the same nature as the body. Now if these two, that which is corporeal and that which is psychic, are both dark, ignorant, harmful and by their nature one, and that they constitute the being and nature of the body, then the question is: what is the substance and nature of the spirit (*gyan*) itself? ... It is of different substance from the body, and is so mixed and bound up with the soul of the body, with wrath and greed and sensuality in the body, as ... The spirit is amalgamated with the power and corporeality of the body, bones, flesh, skin, breath ... by the fetter of the soul (*menog*) of the body (*tan*).

The fivefold influence will therefore be considered from the aspects of the bodily elements, soul and spirit respectively.

The five pure elements of the kingdom of light, with which Primal Man armed himself for his descent, were ether, wind, light, water and fire (p. 13). These are known as *amahraspandan* or Amshaspands. They are the Regents of Time, who with their opposites are expressed in the passage of the sun through the zodiac in the course of the year.[1]

The corresponding elements of the realm of darkness

were smoke (namely, the poison of death), flame, scorching wind, water (or suffocating fumes), and darkness. Each of these elements was inhabited, and led by an archon: darkness by reptiles, led by a dragon; water by swimming things, led by a fish; wind by flying things, led by an eagle; fire (i.e. blood warmth) by quadrupeds, led by a lion; and smoke was inhabited by bipeds, led by a demon, namely, the Prince of Darkness himself, who was a monster with the head of a lion, the body of a dragon, wings of a bird, the tail of a fish, and the feet of a beast of burden.

The Manichaeans related the four basic elements to the four quarters of the earth in a manner similar to the Greeks,[2] except that because of the different location of Babylonia the east was regarded as wet (Indian Ocean, monsoons) and the west as dry (Arabian and Egyptian deserts). Thus, for example, the north-west related to the earth element (cold and dry) and thus to the Ram, Lion and Archer; whereas for the Greeks it related to water (cold and wet) and hence to Crab, Scorpion and Fishes. In view of his many journeys and his clairvoyance, this will have been for Mani an intimate experience, not the abstract idea it appears to us.

He was not however satisfied with this, and also related the five elements of darkness to the zodiac in an ingenious and unique manner. This is best shown diagrammatically:

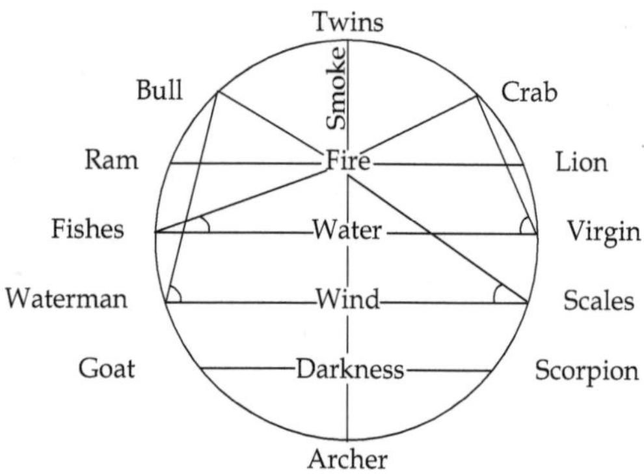

Taking the five signs from Scorpion to Fishes as the dark realm corresponding to winter and to the limbs and lower body, this shows a clear progression: the element of darkness relates to two dark signs; smoke to one dark and one light; water and wind to one dark and two light; and fire to two light signs. There is also a certain feeling of symmetry.

The choice of the vertical axis of Twins and Archer for 'smoke' (i.e. the poison of death) is significant. This is the polarity of midday/midsummer and midnight/midwinter respectively, the contrasting seasons. From the Twins come the positive/negative forces of electricity and earth magnetism, and also the forces of radioactivity, which bring death into western consciousness. From the Archer come the duality between the higher soul qualities and the lower animal astrality, which is liable to misuse in the East. The best forces work in the central horizontal polarity of Fishes (love) and Virgin (tact of heart), which are here combined with the Crab (purification) in relation to water, bearer of the etheric realm.[3] But the full significance of this whole relationship is not yet clear.

Turning to the spiritual qualities, the 'dwellings' or 'limbs' forming the apprehensible body of the Father of Greatness (or of Light) were said to be: Nous, mind, intelligence, thought and understanding. These are also found personalized as the Sons of the Living Spirit, namely:

- The Holder of Glory, who stands with six faces and radiant with light between the fixed and the wandering stars (Nous)
- The King of Honour, who in the seventh heaven, surrounded by cohorts of angels, judges the demons of the abyss (mind)
- The Adamas of Light, belligerent, with spear in his right hand and brazen shield in his left, who treads earth's trembling foundation in the midst of the world (intelligence)

- The King of Glory, who turns the wheels of winds, water and living fire in the abyss (thought).
- The Bearer (Atlas), who on bended knee supports the earth with both hands, and carries the burden of the creation (understanding).

The substance of Primal Man is the same. Another text speaks of gentleness, knowledge, understanding, silence and penetration.

The dark counterpart of this is not at the level of spirit but at that of the body, where the work of the demon of desires gave rise to bones, muscles, veins, flesh and skin.

At the intermediate level of soul were also found (p. 29), among the twelve hours of the demon of desire, the qualities translated as hatred, obduracy, instinctiveness, impatience and stupidity. The qualities of the soul's 'harkening' to the 'call' directly correspond: love, faith, perfecting (or fidelity), perseverance (or bravery) and wisdom. It may be permissable to interpret the polarity of hatred and love as a working of Venus; obduracy and faith as that of Mercury; instinct and perfecting as that of Saturn; impatience and perseverance as that of Mars; and stupidity and wisdom as a working of Jupiter.

We can now grasp another fundamental tenet of Manichaeism, which divided human evolution into three stages: the first, while Primal Man was still in the kingdom of light; then the long period of time when light is intermingled with darkness; and a third still in the far future, when light and darkness will again be separated, but darkness will no longer be able to attack the light. The picture now emerges of the way in which Primal Man was fettered to the body by means of the adverse soul qualities, and how through harkening to the awakening call, filled as it now is by the impulse of the Jesus of Light, not only is the soul freed again from the body but a higher spiritual stage than before is attained. This stage is called the New Man, the Light Self, or the Son of Righteousness; it is equivalent to the Second Adam described by Paul. The whole progress may be tabulated as follows:[4]

Primal Man	*Fettered by*	*Into*	*Awakening Call*	*New Man*
Nous	Hatred	Bones	Love	Spirit core
Mind	Obduracy	Muscles	Faith	Inner thinking
Intelligence	Instinctiveness	Veins	Perfecting	Inner life
Thought	Impatience	Flesh	Perseverence	Right relation to world
Understanding	Stupidity	Skin	Wisdom	Harmony with world in knowledge and action

Mani's qualities assigned to the New Man can be recognized in Steiner's description of how, after making moral ideals living and strong, it is possible to develop along a path of wonder, reverence, feeling in wisdom-filled harmony with the world, and surrender to the course of the world.[5]

Although many details are difficult to understand, it is clear that the fundamental process is one of degeneration into the body followed by self-development or transformation (the *metanoie* of the New Testament, usually mistranslated by the banal 'repentance'). There is no mention here of sense-nerve or rhythmic systems, only aspects of the limbs influenced by the earth, the foundation of the will. It is clear that Manichaeism contained a path of initiation or self-development (which may be why it was attacked so strongly by Rome and other priesthoods who wished to keep all esotericism to themselves). Sayings such as the following confirm this:

- The gentleness of the Holy Spirit will in truth open your inner sense, so that you behold your own soul with your very eyes.
- The apostle said: He appears not to these bodily eyes, but is found by the eyes of the mind.

- In this sphere love is king, love is the source of all good actions, it is like the radiant sun which surpasses all lights, it is like the tree that bears the best fruits; he who has love has through it also the highest principle; love and faith are for all saints the basis for the development to light, the wonderful door through which everything is to be seen.
- Receive the yoke of meekness—meekness has overcome death and enslaved the enemy.
- Unless you make the things of the right hand as those on the left, and the things of the left hand as those on the right, and those that are above as those below, and those that are behind as those before you, you shall not have knowledge of the kingdom.

7
Manichaean Community Life

Mani centred his community in the ancient Chaldean city of Babylon, near his birthplace, and its centre remained there until forced by Islamic persecution in the tenth century to withdraw beyond the Oxus to Samarkand. The task of Chaldean worship of Ea (Sophia), Marduk (Michael) and the planetary gods had been to connect the ensouled being of the cosmos with the realm of nature through astronomy, mathematics and natural law;[1] and Mani introduced this into his community. Augustine said that they commanded no one to believe until the truth had first been discussed and then explained.

Mani's followers called themselves simply Christians—it was only the Church that referred to them as Manichaeans. Augustine was impressed by the cordiality of this 'intimate circle of serious-minded friends'—especially when soon after he reached Rome his host helped him recuperate from a serious illness. They held freedom of conscience as essential, and could thus never recognize a 'state religion' (though once had to accept it).

Since Mani aimed at universality, especially for adherents of the eastern Mysteries, it is quite understandable that he removed from the Gospel texts all references to the Old Testament and to baptism. (His followers complained that Abraham called his wife his sister and gave her to a foreign king as mistress; Lot committed incest; David took a general's wife; Solomon was polygamous; and Moses was not only a murderer but cursed everyone that 'hangs on a tree' or 'raised not a seed', both of which applied to Jesus.) Augustine complained that 'they speak evil of the patriarchs and prophets, and say that the law given by God's servant Moses was not given by God but by the Prince of

Darkness'. Steiner, however, once called Manichaeism 'a remarkable formula for overcoming the old heathenism at the same time as the Old Testament'.[2]

To maintain his community after his death 'until the end', so that souls from other religions who 'have not accomplished the work' would be able to find the door of redemption later through reincarnation, Mani organized an ongoing hierarchy of five levels. This consisted of twelve Masters or Teachers, sons of gentleness; 72 Bishops, sons of knowledge; 360 Priests, sons of reason; the Elect (both male and female), sons of secrets; and the Hearers, sons of insight.

Hearers might eat meat, possess property or wealth, and marry or keep a mistress (as did Augustine), but were advised not to have children. They prayed four times daily, and all fasted on Sundays. On Mondays they made confession to the Elect (who also fasted then) under 15 headings. Their sins were regarded as an involuntary and temporary loss of consciousness, for which confession, contrition and renewed awareness were sufficient atonement (but there was no repentance for refusal to recognize that evil had independent existence). They were enjoined to walk in truth, to love other Hearers as brothers in the living family, and to avoid all forms of evil. They both loved and feared the Elect, begging on their knees (according to Augustine) the imposition of their hands, and joining them in praying to sun and moon.

Mani's teaching that particles of light were mingled in all matter led to a remarkable environmentalism. His followers had to avoid (or confess) any damage not only to animals but to plants, trees, even soil, water or fire. 'Like a highwayman who kills are all of you who lay hands on the earth and torture it in every way. With your whole body you move over the earth and wound it; this living self from which you were born you violate and injure, it continually weeps and complains. How many times are you in need of absolution and mercy!'

Absolution had obviously to be given to those Hearers whose task was the preparation of food. At the daily ritual meal the Elect even began with an apology to the bread: 'I did not mow thee, nor grind thee, nor knead thee, nor bake thee—another did this for me; I eat thee without sin.' This was no mere selfish asceticism, but a question of purification, so that the light of the plant might be redeemed by them back to the realm of light. They realized that only through man can the earth be redeemed; and because they kept the Three Seals (below), the elect were the earthly agents for this through their digestive systems. The cult of bread-giving was on one hand a social recognition of the needs of others who hunger. It was also however a contemplation of the plant, in whose growth and colour the light was seen as a path to the cosmic life-soul of Primal Man; and its binding to the earth was experienced as Jesus the Sufferer. The participant who cut the corn or ate the bread was thus to feel himself as dark, selfish, and in need of the light, the sacrifice of the Light King; therefore he must work on himself as the stars work on the corn, to achieve a transubstantiation in vision, in creativity, and in work.[3]

In one of his letters Mani wrote:

> Do not bear witness, nor swear an oath time and again, nor make others swear ... Do not speak in an irritated and confused manner, and let not a word of destruction go forth from your mouth, for it is of the destructive word that a bloody demoness is born ... Soothe one another, and build each other up, and dispel each other's sorrows, and be dear to one another in kindness, and always run with these secrets and edify each other ...

On the other hand, Hearers were commanded to renounce worship of idols; lying; greed; killing; fornication; theft; teaching of pretences, including false witness and the extension of truth; sorcery; holding two opinions about religion; sickness and negligence in work.

Stricter standards still were required of the Elect, who were dedicated to the redemption of the soul as well as to the reunification of light; and all deeds that did not free light from matter were forbidden them. Since God was considered to be one with human souls, human salvation was also God's redemption. But if the moral code lapsed, God was directly affected, so every sin was also blasphemy—this was very burdensome.

On appointment the Elect were anointed with oil, baptism as a sacrament being inconceivable. They prayed seven times daily, and had to observe three Seals of Righteousness:

- The Seal of the Mouth, which covered both cleanliness of thought and word (namely, freedom from desire) and the eating only of plants, oil and fruits (melons and olives were considered a special gift of Paradise) but not wine.
- The Seal of the Hands, namely, avoiding all harm to light particles (e.g. bathing was forbidden because it defiled the water) and carrying feeling and morality into every activity, such as art, handwork, or work as a scribe. Material riches were seen as a prison, so that anyone who built a house must care for at least one other person who could not otherwise live—or he would suffer their homelessness.
- The Seal of the Breast, namely, the overcoming of inherited sin, and the relinquishment of sex, marriage and possessions. The opposite sex were to be treated as a craftsman treats fire, without letting it burn him.

In the East these three Seals were replaced by 'Five Commandments': i) purity of mouth, ii) avoiding injury to anything, iii) purity of body, iv) blessed poverty, v) truthfulness. Whether wandering as preachers or living in monasteries, the Elect were dependent on the gifts of laymen, who would collect 'merit' by what was termed 'soul-service to their own souls' thereby.

The Elect underwent before death ritual purification (probably with holy water) in the hope of returning to the realm of light. Since a principal object of Mani's religion was to free the light-soul from the body, death was regarded as something good. Mourning and lamentation were therefore sins, and funerals were superfluous. There is a parable about a woman 'who up to now did not know that if I mourn about the bodily son I kill the spiritual son. But from now on I will not weep and kill him.'

As soon as the soul of the righteous left the body, it beheld its redeemer and saviour, the twin who was always within, even if unknown in life. It rose with the image of its master and the three angels with him on a column of light as far as the moon. There it came before the judge of truth, Jesus the Judge, and received the victory. Eighty angels of the opposite sex exhorted the righteous to stride forward into the Paradise of Light and taste its joy. The soul met its higher self as a wonderful divine virgin personifying its earthly deeds, whose character and appearance was influenced by its own behaviour. Since good deeds were a treasure, the higher self was 'the treasurer'; and certain Elect were 'treasurers of the glorious Mother', who accompanied the soul to Paradise and real life. Perfect Hearers were also able to receive complete salvation after death. But other Hearers were subject to 'reforging', to be steeled again by fire, first in the light element of fruits, then in the bodies of the Elect, before regaining the realm of light. 'Even Hearers will be immortal', while those not awakened by the Nous are after individual judgment placed on the left and return as beasts.

At the festivals, hymns were sung to special tunes:

> Sing out beautifully and gladly the wonderful hymn 'To salvation, peace and faith'. Blow the trumpet that makes glad, 'Lead souls together for salvation'. Joyfully come the sons of gods at the voice of this delightful song. Say: Holy, Holy. Call

> out: Amen, Amen. Ring out 'The Light of Wisdom'. Respond with holy speech 'The Life Word of Truth sets loose the Bound One from his Bond'. Prepare the soul for purification, and keep in holiness this true mystery.

Two long hymn-cycles have been preserved. The Hearers were required not only to be present but to participate in such festivals.

At a festival that evoked the course of the year, the Principal, in radiant ether-red, was surrounded by twelve Masters. Day spirits brought what the elements have wrested from light; year-gods brought the good achieved during the year. Heavenly beings endowed the freed and strengthened souls with power, each Aeon giving a different capacity. The beautiful, good and healed returned to heaven with garlands and songs of praise—the earth had thrown off its dead crust.

The important annual Bema (communion) festival was a commemoration of Mani's death, and was preceded by a month's fast. Hearers confessed to Mani their sins during the year and asked for forgiveness. The Seal letter was then read, and hymns sung to Mani himself as well as to the other gods of the drama, 'the bright gods, the praised elements of light, the soul-gathering angels, those that receive the Living Self. May they themselves accept from us this hymn, as well as praise and prayer and good works, the fruit and aid of the bright Nous.'

A picture (see book cover) shows the Principal, with hand raised in blessing, sitting beside a tripod with melons on it; a priest is kneeling before a table holding loaves; and the Elect, robed in white with auras like chef hats, are sitting either side of a throne or rostrum. This was carpeted but empty, because no declaration *ex cathedra* was needed, for Christ was always present in each heart (this was common in the East). After the Hearers had departed, the Elect sprinkled their heads with olive oil and prayed to 'the very strong powers, the very best gods', reciting many names. Most prominent among these was 'Jesus the Splendour, the Vivifier, the New Aeon, true Raiser of the Dead'. A specimen hymn to him will be found in Appendix 5.

8
The Expansion and Contraction of Manichaeism

Mani organized extensive missionary activity in his lifetime, especially to Egypt (Adda, first bishop 261), and his movement reached Rome and southern Gaul during the fourth century. But a revolt against the empire in Egypt was supposed to have been stirred by Manichaeans, and the movement was forbidden by decree of Diocletian in 302. Although this was probably annulled eleven years later, opposition from the Roman Church from 312 onwards was such that its members were at one time required even to curse Mani; so his religion vanished from the west of the empire in the fifth century and from the east of it in the sixth. A small group continued however in North Africa, survived the Vandal onslaught of 439, and lasted until the eighth century. They seem to have adopted a monastic style there even before the Christians; from them originated the Coptic texts.

In the Arian/Athanasian controversy of 325, Athanasius, who held a position closer to Manichaeism, was defeated. The emperor Julian the Apostate, already an initiate of the Eleusinian Mysteries, was actually on his way to receive the Persian initiation which was in harmony with Manichaeism concerning Christ Jesus, the overcoming of evil, and the future of the earth, when he was assassinated by Constantine Christians in 363.[1]

Augustine belonged to the community in Egypt from 376 to 382, when their teaching had already been Romanized and dogmatized to such an extent that it could no longer be fully understood.[2] (The Coptic psalms, for example, are almost orthodox.) So long as he could see clairvoyantly how Christ descended from divine spheres to dwell in the flesh, and how with Him the riddle of evil was solved, Augustine was impressed. But as his intellect developed he found them 'more clever and quick-witted in refuting others than firm and sure in proof of what is their own'. Bishop Faustus could not convince him of the unity of spirit and matter, and he thought (erroneously) that Mani had taught that evil was as eternal as good, and that there was no resurrection of the body; so he turned to Rome.[3] By an edict of Theodosius in 381 Manichaeism was again proscribed, now retrospectively.

Persecution also in Persia in the mid-fifth century led many adherents to flee to Armenia. There they merged with the Gnostic Nestorian Christians, who shared the view that the Jesus born of Mary could not be the Son of God, and were declared heretical in 431. Since the second century they had built churches with a distinctive square cupola and vaulted arches, and now in developing Nisibis as the official market on the Silk Road to China, they incorporated the barrel roof. The Goths, with the inner experience of Christ in their hearts, had already reached Rome in 410, and called on Armenians to help build their capital at Ravenna. That is how in the southern mosaics of San Vitali we find, accompanying Jesus, a mysterious figure in white representing the Manichaean conception of the cosmic Christ. When Rome regained control, the Armenian style of church was preferred to the Roman temple tradition, despite their heretical beliefs. Many Armenians, Manichaeans among them, settled in Lombardy, where they had many schools and adherents, and from there free student communities spread north of the Alps. Gradually these masons, independent of Rome's control, spread across Europe, until in the age of cathedral-building they dominated the scene as free masons.[4]

Meanwhile a Manichaean centre had formed in Bactra (probably modern day Balkh, now Wazirabad) in the fifth century; and when the caravan routes of the Silk Road were reopened by China in the late sixth century, the movement (and Nestorianism) spread eastwards along the northern Tarim route. Since the Elect would refuse to be carried by any animal, they probably worked mainly in the merchants' compounds. A 'Compendium of Doctrines' of 731 from here is extant. In Uighur in the Takla Makan (from where the Indian, Persian and Egyptian cultures had earlier been founded) Manichaeism was the state religion of the Turks from 760 to 840. This was a mainly Buddhist area, and Mani was presented here as 'the Buddha of Light'; hence the movement took on the form of Buddhist monasticism, which favoured its artistic development. Chinese texts found here are translated into Buddhist formulations.

Freedom of worship was also granted in China itself, specifically for foreigners only, from 732 to 843. Here Mani was presented as a reincarnation of Lao-tzu, the founder of Taoism, and two of his works were incorporated into the Taoist canon. Manichaeism survived under persecution, especially in Fukien (South China), until the sixteenth century, its texts being remarkably faithful to those further west. All this was achieved without any military force.

In the seventh century in Asia Minor, Manichaeism united with the Paulicians, who held to the Luke Gospel and the letters of Paul, but rejected the Old Testament and the hierarchy and sacraments of the Church. They spread to Thrace, especially to Philippopolis (present-day Plovdiv in Bulgaria), about 750. Here, in common with the Bogomils (Friends of God), founded in the tenth century, the teaching of 'no matter without spirit'—known in Greece since Aristotle—was emphasized. Steiner gives a vivid picture of the Bogomil's imaginative life, and their feeling that during sleep their inner being belonged to regions of good and evil.[5] They were later driven by the Huns to Bosnia. The mediaeval mystics of central Europe also called themselves 'Friends of God'.

The twelfth century saw the emergence of the Cathars or Albigenses in northern Italy and southern France (catharsis: purification). With their 'Good Men' or elect, they held the view that the body is intrinsically evil, and cannot be the creation of a good God. Their connection with Manichaeism, suspected but unproven, is affirmed by Steiner, who says the same of the Templars[6]—they sought to sustain Christianity in the East, and to carry the esoteric impulse of the Grail into the secular task of leading evil back to good. All these movements were ruthlessly suppressed at the instigation of the Church and the Inquisition, so that by the end of the Middle Ages even these last vestiges of Manichaeism were extinct.

However, the inner spirit of the Manichaeans remained alive in isolated groups; and Manichaean souls of course reincarnate. Whereas the Church also opposed the heathen cultures of classical Greece and Rome, the Renaissance impulse to renew them may have been prepared by such souls. Whether and to what extent they contributed to the Reformation also awaits research. The name of Faustus echoed on in corrupt form in the legend of Faust, for example in Marlowe. In Goethe's drama it is characteristic that Faust does not fight evil overtly; instead he makes a pact with Mephistopheles—indeed, the fundamental question is how Mephistopheles is to be redeemed.[7] Goethe, like Mani, regarded darkness not as a mere absence of light, as does Newton, but as a separate active principle. His basic observation with a prism shows unequivocally how colour arises through the reciprocal interweaving of the two, not just from the light.

In the twentieth century a Manichaean impulse may be found in the work of Albert Steffen, for example in this poem:[8]

Within this pain so deep,
By sheaths of destiny protected,
There sprouts a germ of joy
Lent by the Risen One.

You will to let it grow
To many forms of life,
So that their blossoming
May flood the Word with light.
You may not, for another,
Unseal the primal abyss
(That is merely naive)
Unless at last of itself
The veil is torn apart.

Why? You well may ask.
O Friend!
In your opponent too,
Though hidden, lives the light.
Though now he sullies truth,
Yet darkness in his soul
Will one day become light.
Then will he cry with shame,
Sink to the earth, confess.
So would you steal from him
His chosen deed of freedom?
Within this pain so deep . . .

(Translated from the German by the author.)

9
Mani's Individuality

As a result of his spiritual research, Rudolf Steiner was able to give indications of seven successive incarnations of the individuality who appeared as Mani. One might have been tempted to start by identifying Mani with Manu, the leader of the Sun-oracle on ancient Atlantis, who led those with the first beginnings of a thinking capacity across to central Asia, where the cultures of India, Persia and Egypt were nurtured. But Steiner does *not* indicate this; on the contrary, he warns that in olden times any great lawgiver and leader of masses of people who had brought Manas (spirit-self) to expression within him would have been called a Manu.[1] Such men are of course rare.

The earliest incarnation to which Steiner refers[2] is that of the Disciple of Sais (in Coptic: Twin) in Egypt. Isis represents there the soul, the mother who receives the divine into herself and conceives. But Osiris, the divine father, has withdrawn, so the female element is no longer confronted by the divine fructifier, and is called 'the widow'. The Disciple tried while still unprepared to lift the veil on her statue that no 'mortal' had yet lifted, to become like the initiates a 'son of the widow'. Seeking to behold unprepared the secrets of the archetypal forces of man and nature, he unveiled the image of Isis on the physical plane, and had to succumb to death. No mortal, no one not prepared by initiation, might at that time lift the veil of Isis. In him is symbolized the wisdom of Egypt, which had by then lost its power.[3]

He then incarnated as one of the three Magi from the East, who brought the old treasures of wisdom of the Indian, Persian and Egyptian ages to the feet of the newborn Jesus, that it might in due time be permeated by the forces of

Christ and thus be made fruitful for mankind's future. As Caspar the Moor from Africa he presented the myrrh, symbol of the death and resurrection of Osiris, of the dying of the lower life and the resurrection of the higher by means of the deep forces of the will. The Magi 'returned to their own country by another way', namely, through death.[4]

He was very soon reborn as the Youth of Nain, who was one of the three raised from death by Christ (Luke 7:11). Now literally son of a widow, he was being carried out of the city gate when Christ Jesus approached. 'And a large crowd from the city were with his mother,' namely, the Egyptian initiates, who bury the dead. 'And when the Lord saw her He had compassion on her', who represented the earthly Isis. 'And He said: young man, I say unto you, arise. And the dead one sat up and began to speak; and He gave him to his mother. And those around glorified God, saying: A great prophet is arisen among us.' This was an initiation of a very special kind, in the depths of the will; it contained the mystery of the working of Christ into the future. Only a seed was planted in his soul, so that he had to wait until the next incarnation for its forces to blossom in him as an initiate, and become a mighty teacher of religion who is gradually to permeate Christianity with the teaching of reincarnation and karma.[5]

Then came the incarnation as Mani from AD 216 to 277. This background enables us to understand why he saw it as his task to draw together the wisdom of the East and transform it through the forces of Christ, and how he gained such strong forces for the future transformation of evil. He now describes himself as 'son of the widow' because he is preparing for the stage when people will lay aside all outer authority, and seek for their own spirit light by gazing into their own souls.[6]

In the fourth century—the central turning-point of the whole post-Atlantean epoch—Mani gathered around him the personalities in whom the mighty individualities of

Zarathustra and Skythianos were then living and in whom Buddha was reflected. Mani himself was a still higher and more powerful individuality than these, now a very high messenger of Christ. This was one of the greatest assemblies of the spiritual world connected with the earth that ever took place, visible only to spiritual sight. Its purpose was to consider how to transform the Mystery wisdom of the pre-Christian cultures so that a real understanding of Christ would gradually become possible.[7] Account will have been taken of the fact that the Folk Spirit of the Celtic peoples had become the Spirit of Esoteric Christianity.[8] The outcome was such that Steiner could say that Christian occultism is derived from Manichaeism.[9]

Then in the ninth century, just at the time when the Roman Church was denying the separate existence of the spirit, Mani incarnated as the historical Parzival,[10] again son of a widow. Parzival prepared in advance the initiation necessary for the Age of the Consciousness Soul,[11] later expressed in the legends by Chrétien, Wolfram and others. These begin in the East with Gahmuret, and have many references to black and white, light and dark. For example, Herzeleide teaches him that God is brighter than daylight, and the master of hell is black. He innocently receives what he is told, but learns at the Grail Castle the need to take interest in another and to question. The recurring *pietà* scene with Sigune recalls the Crucifixion, which the Youth of Nain (who remained a follower of Christ[12]) is likely to have witnessed. While Gawain fights on behalf of little Obilot, Parzival is on the other side seeking to transform the aggressor. He comes to Christ through developing his own inner forces. On becoming Lord of the Grail his half-brother Fierefiz from the East is brought to Christianity. His successor (after Lohengrin) is Prester John.

Mani was again in incarnation when in 1459 he initiated Christian Rosencreutz into a true understanding of the nature of evil.[13] At this time the reborn Seven Rishis, representing the wisdom of Atlantis and representatives of the four post-Atlantean cultures, united to pour their wisdom into the young Rosencreutz. So Mani's task in relation to the past flowed into the Rosicrucian movement,[14] and he was then able to concentrate on his task for the future. In the Rosicrucian school, the four who met in the fourth century were the teachers. It is difficult to distinguish their respective contributions, but the teaching 'to slip into the skin of the dragon' is peculiarly Manichaean.

Steiner has not indicated any subsequent incarnation, but there may nevertheless have been one in the nineteenth century who was known to him. He is reported as saying that Mani would not incarnate in the twentieth century, but intends to do so in the twenty-first, if he can find a suitable body and also have a Waldorf education. He would then stand forth as a teacher of mankind, and take over leadership in the realms of art and religion, working in the strength of the Grail mystery, and leading people to decide for themselves between good and evil.[15]

10
The Future Role of Manichaeans

In deeply moving words Rudolf Steiner has depicted from various aspects the increasing and necessary role of evil in human evolution. Evil as well as good forces are today still within us, as the animals once were; and just as we have freed ourselves from the animal, so shall we in the course of future incarnations wrest ourselves free from evil. The tragic aspect is that one class of beings must first abase itself that the other may rise. But Christ washed the feet of the disciples; and for Manichaeans to achieve their aim of refining human beings and become redeemers, the master must become the servant of all.[1]

Serious account must be taken of the fact that mankind has now crossed the Threshold into the spiritual world. New forces are available for spiritual development, but if instead they are misapplied for selfish ends on this side of the Threshold they work destructively as cruelty, treachery and so on. Henceforth everyone will feel urged by the Double within him to think materialistically, and those who rely only on instinct and intelligence will increasingly bring about evil results.[2] Mani said of this: 'To you I speak, my captive souls: remember your real home, the hard battles of old, and the many battles you have had with darkness. Remember the middle line of the Threshold, and the boundary of the two spheres.'

We have seen that forces which can work for either good or ill originate in the cosmos; that is to say, they are inherent in our astral bodies, although we only know their reflection into the physical and etheric bodies as deeds or thoughts. Good tendencies can therefore be inherited from parents through the sentient body, and be developed up to puberty into excellent and noble inclinations to do what is right and good. At puberty the astral body is freed from the parental sheath, and astral forces from the previous incarnation enter. If the young person does not think about the moral problems these different forces raise, then his (or her) own children will not inherit the good instincts, but be uncertain in their moral life; nor will he in his next life bring decisive instincts for good. Hence morality develops in the family environment, and the good ones will increasingly be separated from the evil. That is why in the sixth (Russian) cultural age it will be necessary to deal with good and evil 'races' (which have nothing whatever to do with the races of today based on inheritance).[3] Moreover people will then be born with countenances that express their inner moral or immoral qualities, so that these will be immediately visible to others. For those who have done wrong this will be an almost fatal destiny, which neither education nor religion will be able to alter.[4] It will be accompanied for them by a falling back into a kind of group soul, which will direct how they should think, feel and act.[5] Misuse of the sexual organs, which by then will have begun to the superseded, will lead to a prevailing vice of indecency, lewdness or lasciviousness, which makes the development of meditation impossible.

The task of the Manichaean stream will at that time be to form and lead communities of those who have turned to the spirit, and who look on love, peace and passive resistance to evil as their normal standard of behaviour, seeking through kindness and charitableness to draw the evil ones back into the progressive stream. Everything from the past that has become rigid, such as the religions of all ages, will have to be brought into harmony with the progressive forces of true Christianity. Individuals must come to be guided out of their own nature by the light of their own souls.[6]

According to Mani, the peace of the invisible God and a knowledge of truth will be with those who believe in the laws of heaven, even as they put them into practice in their daily lives. We saw in Chapter 7 how strict were the laws of behaviour in Mani's own community. The linking of cosmic life with human life and destiny in this way was deeply rooted within the Manichaeans, who shunned the evil everywhere in life.[7] This goes so deep that a growing number of people will become able, at the moment of a new incarnation when they take their karma into their new etheric body, to realize how gravely they have harmed someone else (as we are always in danger of doing) and to decide to give him the body they have prepared for themselves, taking on instead and redeeming that of the other. Without this impulse, the earth will never be able to reach its goal.[8] The turning of the other cheek can now be seen as a first preparation for this.

The end of the whole post-Atlantean epoch in the seventh age will bring even greater changes for mankind. Reproduction as we know it will no longer be possible, and egoism in the struggle to survive will turn to destruction in the War of All against All. Only a few who have acquired the courage to develop a quite different consciousness will be carried over by the force of redemption to repopulate the next main epoch.[9] It is hardly surprising that those who have made no effort towards perfection will be filled with envy (Chapter 5).

Rudolf Steiner mentioned a Manichaean school or order which was training its members so that they may be able in later generations to transform evil into good. They know that some day there will be those in whose karma there is no longer any evil, but also a race evil by nature, among whom all kinds of evil will be developed to a higher degree than in the most savage animals. But he sternly warns that Mani's initiation and all it entails must remain carefully hidden for a long time to come yet, or harm will result, not good.[10] Mani's statement that he is inspired by the Paracelete means that he is preparing for this time. Hence he laid stress on purity of both mind and life—his particular task is less a cultivation of the inner life than of the outer forms of life.[11]

In the new epoch described in the Apocalypse as that of the Seals, the lofty Manichaean principle will win more and more pupils. They will have to make strenuous efforts to rescue the evil ones, who will not resemble bad children in whom good waits to be drawn out but will practise evil consciously, exquisitely, with the help of highly developed intellects. But there will also be those gifted with mighty inner forces of good, the greatest love; and precisely through their transforming of the former will a quite special good, a moral holiness, unfold on earth.[12] The Manichaean stream, which goes beyond Rosicrucianism, will then express Christianity in its most complete form.[13]

The end of the world is heralded in Manichaeism as in Mark 13 and Matt. 24–25.

> The false Mithra, whose mount is a bull and whose token is war, will appear as part of a great war. The 'new generation' will come and take firm possession of its estate. Then Jesus will assume dominion as the Great King, and souls will appear before his judgment seat at the centre of the world. The Hearers will be placed at his right hand, while the sinners on his left will be cast into hell. The Elect will be changed into angels, and the Jesus of Light will then leave with them for the realm of light.
>
> The last particles of light that can be rescued will be raised by the Instinct of Life in a cosmic pillar of light. At a sign from Jesus the five sons of the Living Spirit who hold up the universe will leave their posts, the entire universe will collapse, and a great fire will burn for 1468 years (compare the scientific picture of entropy and the warmth-death of the universe). Az and Ahriman, with the damned and demons—matter and darkness—will be thrown into a shapeless clod, sunk in the cosmic moat, covered with a gigantic rock, and bound for ever without end in that prison. Light and darkness will again be distinct, as in the beginning.

Augustine complained that according to Mani God would be unable even at the end of the world to get Himself wholly cleansed. But the Manichaeans took a longer view.

> The Gods will not sorrow over that part of light which cannot be separated from darkness, for sorrow is not for them. On the contrary, since they have subdued Ahriman and his enmity, and bound him in a prison of oblivion over which they rule, their mind is joyous, blissful and happy, because nobody can harm them any longer. That sinner who boasted deceitfully and fought with the Father of Greatness has been seized and bound up in an extraordinary tomb out of which he can never escape. And the earth, the abode of the foes, the house of darkness, is thrown into confusion and levelled. And over it the Gods of Light have erected the bright foundation of the New Aeon.

Steiner indeed speaks of later possibilities of redemption.[14] He explains that it is Lucifer and Ahriman themselves who relegate unalloyed evil to the so-called 'Eighth Sphere'.[15] But the Manichaeans knew that even at a future stage of Earth evolution (the fifth 'Condition of Life'), when there is no longer a mineral kingdom, there would still be two groups of human beings, the good and the bad. They therefore already made it their task to educate people so that then too they might become educators of the kingdom of evil men. A deeper profundity is thus seen again and again in the Manichaeans.[16]

Conclusion

Mani was an incarnation of an individuality of the highest importance for human evolution. He had been initiated by Christ Himself in a unique way into the depths of the will, enabling him to undertake a special task in the overcoming of evil, leading into the far future. Directly inspired by the Holy Spirit, he founded a new religion containing the seeds of Christianity in a form that aimed not only to renew the high pre-Christian cultures in a manner fruitful for the rest of the post-Atlantean epoch and on into the epoch of the Seals, but also to redeem nature itself through the spirit which he experienced as light.

He realized that darkness and evil were of cosmic origin, and could therefore only be transformed through exertion of the corresponding cosmic good, whereas the attempt to eliminate evil by force would inevitably create new negative karma to be overcome. His method was neither philosophical nor theological, but mythical, artistically creative and experiential; it was not based on the sword or punishment, but mild and gentle. He did not seek to impose dogmatic beliefs, but to establish in habits of practical behaviour a middle way between Az and Ahriman through which people could find their own paths to freedom. He taught that only through human understanding, loving behaviour and sacrifice could the power of Jesus Christ achieve its aim.

Despite a wide following, his purpose was frustrated by the established religions. So in his next life he set in train a new impulse of Christian esotericism that was to grow out of the inner nature of each individual. As Parzival he carried further the Grail impulse, so that in the Age of the Consciousness Soul it might flourish in Rosicrucianism, the direct precursor of anthroposophy. The special initiation through which he prepares others for the future must at present remain in a very small circle, but after the war of All Against All it will involve very many. It is a path not of killing the dragon but of entering into its skin in order to develop, through transforming its forces, a very special good.

That Mani centred his community in Babylon was no accident but an occult necessity; for Babylon signifies 'the mother of harlots and of earth's abominations' (Rev. 17:5), the centre of black magic and the beast Sorath (666). It is here that Michael as Sun Genius is to overcome the beast with the two horns.[1] This will be the culmination of Mani's task.

He is 'a very high messenger of Christ',[2] whose task ranges across the cultural ages of many Archai. Perhaps his contemporary Uzia the Teacher did not exaggerate when he said at Mani's death (Appendix 2): 'The spirit figure shone forth, for it was of the rank of the Exusiai.' For those six Exusiai known as the Elohim, who 'made man in their own image', are also known as 'Spirits of Light'.[3] They represent six aspects of Christ, the Pleroma or Fullness, who *is* the Light of the World. And they will manifest successively as such during the last three post-Atlantean ages and the first three of the ages of the Seals.[4] We may picture Mani as the rider who has mastered the black horse, the forces of the will, and holds in his hand the scales, through which he finally brings individual karma into balance (Rev. 6:5).

Mani's full significance must remain a mystery for the future to unfold.

Appendix 1
A Note on Mithraism

The Mysteries of Mithra, into which Mani was initiated, belonged to the Egypto-Chaldean (Taurus) age in Persia (though the first mention of Mitra in 1400 BC comes from India). They withdrew after the conquest of Persia by Alexander in 330 BC, but continued in degenerating form. (The emergence of Mithraism in the Roman army after AD 136 was almost a new creation.) These Mysteries provided an inner path of initiation, in contrast to the outer path of Zurvanism, belonging to the Persian (Gemini) age of Zarathustra. The Mithraic path led by means of animal sacrifices to self-knowledge of one's own innermost bodily nature, and thence to secrets of the active forces of the universe which created it.[1]

In the original legend, Mithra was a child of the earth, born bearing a torch and a knife. At the behest of the sun-god, he rode and reluctantly killed the life-giving cosmic bull. Thereupon his cloak became the sky, with fixed stars and planets. The bull became the moon, while its tail and blood gave rise to ears of grain and grapes; and from its genitals ran the holy seed which, received in a mixing bowl, shaped every earthly creature. Awakened by the light, there emerged from the earth creatures of darkness – scorpion, lion and serpent. After banqueting with the sun-god, Mithra mounted his chariot and drove across ocean and air to the end of the world.

The soul was regarded as having descended from heaven through the seven planetary spheres, taking on their vices, until caught in the body; and the task was to reascend, like Mithra in the sun-chariot, back to the fixed stars. Hence there were seven grades of initiation—raven, bridegroom, soldier, lion, Persian, Sun-courier and Father. This corresponded to the path of the soul after death. Each grade had its own planetary god, and its own mask or dress.

Rituals were held in subterranean caverns and required artificial light, a symbol of the inner life. There was always a well, and often a system of passages which could be used in the ritual. There are references to blindfolding and prostration, baptism, freeing from fetters, passwords, gates or steps on a ladder.

As representative of the sun-god who saw everything, Mithra was regarded at the level of religion as the mediator, the god of communication and relations between human beings, and hence of oaths, justice and friendship, but also of war. In particular, he was seen as mediator between Ahura Mazda and Ahriman; human redemption depended upon him. In a hymn of 500 BC he is the arch-foe of the powers of evil and darkness. He is paired with the goddess of fertilizing waters.

A picture is extant showing Mani dressed as a priest of Mithra, in wide yellow-green trousers and a cloak of sky-blue, with an ebony cane. There is also a coin inscribed 'Mani, the appointed of Mithra'.

Appendix 2
Albert Steffen's Drama
The Death Experiences of Manes

The Swiss poet Albert Steffen (1884–1963) wrote two dramas and an essay on Manichaeism. The first drama, *Die Manichaer* (not translated), was performed at the Zurich Stadttheater in 1917, and described the battle between spiritual vision, based on knowledge gained through spiritual activity, and agnosticism, tied to the laws of nature. In 1930 two lectures were published in German as an essay entitled *Mani*. Then in 1933, before many documents now available were known, came the drama with the above title, concerning Mani's personal destiny. In his programme note, after describing Mani's background, Steffen outlined his drama as follows:

> The First Act of my drama opens with the arrival of Mani before the gate of Gundeshapur. He has been summoned to court by Nadhira, the wife of Shapur I, without the king's knowledge, as teacher to the eldest son. Manes witnesses a death sentence pronounced by the king. Nicanor, a philosopher who attacked the Ormuzd cult in his school, is being led out to be crucified. The eldest son cannot resist overwhelming anguish and is in danger of death. Shapur, deeply moved, releases Nicanor and turns to Manes for help, asking him to heal the child and to reconcile Nadhira.
>
> In the Second Act Shapur and Nadhira, strangers because of differences in their race and traditions, seem to find themselves. The king gives a feast in honour of the queen, who comes from India. Dancers and musicians represent her birth—her descent from the starry dwellings of the Devas—and afterwards, at the son's request, whose longing to leave the world is increasing, Buddha's entry into Nirvana. The boy, who is 14, and has received through his teachers Addas, Tamas

and Hermas a knowledge greatly surpassing that of his age, but has the purest and most innocent heart, sees into the net of lies in human relationships. Buddha's teachings of compassion show him the dark depths of his father's soul. He cannot find again the way leading back to life.

Manes considers himself guilty of the boy's death. He could not obliterate through the healing force of the spirit the teaching of the sufferings of the world. He sees in the image of the Widow of Nain's son, who was raised to life by Christ, that he is still unable to overcome the seeds of death. He feels his guilt, consisting in the fact that he has not been true, and is ready to accept Shapur's sentence. At this point Nadhira helps him to escape to Kaskar, where a Christian Council is to take place.

The Third Act sets forth the course of this Council. Manes, who cannot accept a dogmatic Christianity based on power but holds instead to the kingdom not of this world, is banished by Bishop Archelaus. His spiritual gaze goes back to primordial ages when humanity was not as yet split into religions. Noah, who has brought over the Mysteries of the Bread from Atlantean times, and is also the first planter of vineyards, appears to Manes surrounded by his sons, the archetypes of the races who are already pursuing separate directions. The kingly and priestly figure of Melchizedek also appears before the seer's eye—Melchizedek who paved the way from the pre-Christian Mysteries to Golgotha, thus announcing a synthesis on a higher stage through the resurrection of Christ, the New Adam. Manes, proscribed as a heretic, sets out for the East, accompanied by Addas, Tamas and Hermas, who have now become his disciples.

The Fourth Act shows Manes in the country of Simurgia. Here dwell the most beautiful race on earth—Greeks who after the expedition of Dionysos to the East remained behind in Asia. The daughter of their rulers loves Manes, but he renounces her love for the sake of his mission, which leads him back to Gundeshapur. In a rock sanctuary he has gained insight into the mysteries of the elements and the stars. The *terra lucida* and *terra pestifera* rise before his spiritual vision. He looks into the past and future of the earth. And out of the depths where darkness rules, King Shapur arises as a deceased man who needs his help to reach the Light. Manes has had a prophetic vision of death, for Shapur, who wished to see him in order to reconcile himself with him, has died. Now Nadhira calls back Manes.

In the last Act, during a ceremony for the dead in honour of Shapur's second son arranged in the Manichaean spirit as a flower-ritual, Manes and Nadhira and all the priests are surprised by the third son, who has become king. They are all murdered, while the last notes of the Hymn of the World's Reconciliation still re-echo:

Light creative, suffering through creation,
Leads man downward on his earthbound journey,
Stars are stages on this pilgrimage.
Fire that smoulders in the deepest chasms
Purifies his spirit-love for sounds
Calling for a new earth, eagerly.
Hark—they're calling—Demiurge and Sufferer!

Appendix 3
Mani's Last Prayer and Death

'O my Father, see: iron is upon me! O my Father, O Primal Man, hear my voice, hear me, the afflicted!

May the sheaths and veils fall, through my entreaty and prayer.

I call on Christ by name. And angels in glory and brilliance, I call in all your names:

Free my spirit from its captivity, take off my cloak of sorrow, lead me out of this world.

O my Father, O Primal Man, open the door of my prayer, through which my petition rises to the heights:

O hear, Maiden of Light, hear my voice you angels, hear the voice of my petition, and loose my chains.

I throw myself before your countenance, and I come to your exalted abode, O Judge of all worlds!

Hear the prayer of the just, I will implore you with all strength.

O Father of the orphans in truth and husband of grief-stricken widows,

O model of holy practice, hear the voice of the afflicted!

O Jesus the Splendour, my redeemer. O perfect Man, Maiden of Light,

Raise my soul to yourself out of the abyss. Put to shame through your trust those who hate;

You have sent me to this place of darkness.

O spirit power of vastness, O Beinghood of Light,

Draw my spirit from the depths, my soul from the descent;

For the body which you built is nullified amidst this world

Under the persecutions I have suffered for your sake since my childhood.

May your great strength come to me, and your angel, all-powerful messenger, help me,

That I may overcome evil, and lay my shackle to the ground, and give over the house to its master,
For it has fought my spirit and become master in its corporality.
At the will of the cosmic spirit I have kept distant from the world's pleasures from the age of twelve until now,
I have found myself, calling upon you and naming myself with your great name.
Hear the voice of him who is the envoy in the world,
I behold your magnificence, I enter into the land of light, it is you whom I call:
So do not be ashamed of me, answer me, O giver of my life, save my soul from sorrows.'

Thus was his voice heard by the King of Love who had sent him.
His body began to loosen, it moved, and his figure resounded,
His glory began to change, his appearance was transformed, a light appeared from his countenance,
From his figure and from his limbs. His bodily members dissolved like a house that rocks,
Like a cloak that tears, he was already bowed to earth.
He ended his prayer, and his eyes were blinded by the tears that flow in streams,
And his chains crunched. And with him spoke the King of Love, who had heard the voice of lament.
The Perfect Man approached him, the Maiden of Light came,
And angels soared in incessant ranks to lead upward his great soul.
And a voice was perceived which arose resounding over the head of the just,
Who led him upwards to the sphere of heaven:
It is the great Christos who will hasten towards him.

The envoy of light returns home, the pearl of light, who will come out of the storm-tossed sea.
The whole cosmos began to resound, choirs of angels came and held ready the prize of victory.
The spirit figure shone forth, for it is of the rank of the Exusiai.

All this Uzia the Teacher reported.

From: Eugen Roll, *Mani, der gesandte des Lichts*
(translated by the author)

Appendix 4
Cosmic Forces of Vice and Virtue

St Mark records in his Gospel (7:21) that Christ Jesus enumerated twelve 'evil thoughts which come from within, out of the heart of man, and defile the man'. On the other hand, Rudolf Steiner once referred in a restricted circle to a list given by H.P. Blavatsky in English of twelve virtues in relation to the months and the zodiac. He himself extended this list (as shown in Chapter 5) and added that if one conscientiously practices these virtues month by month, starting the next one on the 21st of the month before (i.e. with some overlap) new forces and capacities arise.[1]

These two lists of evil thoughts and virtues can be correlated if the positive and negative are taken, as might be expected, in opposite sequence. In what follows, the connections are briefly examined in the context of other indications given by Steiner concerning the zodiac, for example in *Man in the Light of Occultism, Theosophy and Philosophy*,[2] and in his work with eurythmists,[3] including the 'Twelve Cosmic Moods'.

OCTOBER—SCALES

In the maturing of autumn we enter the inorganic world and the processes of decay and mineralizing, but it would be *foolishness* if our thinking were to be restricted by materialism to this realm. The forces of the Scales bring the possibility of weighing pros and cons in thought until the balance of a true realism is attained. We see that the old must fall away to make room for the new, not only in nature but also in human culture. Sympathetic understanding for destruction as well as growth gives rise to *contentment*. This does not mean being indolently satisfied with whatever happens, but that the vicissitudes of life are seen in the wider context which enables us to face them and accept our karma with the help of the spirit. Contentment thus becomes *equanimity*.

NOVEMBER—SCORPION

In passing from materialism to wisdom we need the help of Lucifer, so that we need to guard against *pride* or arrogance. We tend to see everything different as a poisonous sting—we say that our pride is nettled. We gradually learn that taking such a sting personally harms ourself more than others, but that every situation can be turned to good if we accept it with *patience*. This word has the wonderful connotation of being a patient, suffering and learning from it, so that we come to observe what is actually at work and how it can be handled in freedom. Patience thus becomes *insight*.

DECEMBER—ARCHER

The person who becomes too self-satisfied to recognize fault in himself projects it upon others, leading to *slander*. The Archer participates in the world as a hunter, and in the moral sphere hunts for someone to blame. Only when such aggressiveness is overcome by *control of the tongue* can he begin to see the situation objectively and eliminate his prejudices. Only then can he allow the world itself to speak, so that there can gradually unfold a *feeling for truth*.

JANUARY—GOAT

It is necessary to tame the animal element which surges up within us all, and bend the knee in reverence to the spirit. The man who wants the fruits of this without himself making the effort will suffer from *envy*. His indolence towards the spirit becomes an animal-like fear of the unknown, which can only be mastered with *courage*. It is an inner courage that we need to do battle with Lucifer and Ahriman, which can be found through confidence in the reality of life between death and rebirth. Through the Christmas event it then becomes the *power of redemption*.

FEBRUARY—WATERMAN
If the animal element is not tamed and sub-earthly forces can surge into the unbridled passions and desires, the result is *indecency* or lewdness. In the man of self-respect these forces are dominated by the ego in the form of *discretion*. In doing so the soul finds the need in silence to concentrate its strength on the universal spirit active within. Comparable outwardly to the fresh life of springtime, the source of new life is experienced inwardly as *meditative force*.

MARCH—FISHES
The person who has done wrong tries to cover over their deed to avoid criticism or punishment, and thus turns to *deceit*: in business this can become an end in itself (fraud). The opposite of this deliberate enfolding of oneself in darkness is 'to let your light shine before men' in the form of *magnanimity*, which means not only generosity but greatness of soul. Its open-hearted participation in the world turns first to interest in others, then to understanding, and finally its ideals are expressed through the whole being in deeds of *love*.

APRIL—RAM
The further degradation beyond deceiving another for one's personal benefit is to harm him purely for the self-satisfaction of doing so: *malice* (acts of wickedness). The corresponding virtue is to help a man purely for the sake of helping him, irrespective of any benefit to oneself. This is real *devotion*, in which one grasps the needs of the situation and looks back to the spirit for the moral intuition as to what to do. The ultimate stage of devotion that has become deed is to give up even life itself for the other through *force of sacrifice*—the Easter deed.

MAY—BULL

It was through desire that Lucifer first drew us down into the sense-world, and Buddha emphasized desire as the beginning of all suffering. This is expressed outwardly in *covetousness* or ruthless greed. But if we were instead to renounce the sense-world we should again fall into the realm of Lucifer. We have to find here a certain *balance* of soul. Nevertheless life will always throw us off balance into the arms of either Lucifer or Ahriman, so that we must as often strive through our own effort with the help of Christ to regain balance—and that way we achieve *progress,* the direction forwards.

JUNE—TWINS

When covetousness turns from goods to people, we come to *acts of adultery,* breaking up a harmony which two people have achieved together. This divisive force of the Twins works against brotherhood by means of egoism, and eventually in the War of All Against All, the evil of the West. The positive aspect of forces from the Twins is a capacity for action and the conviction that one will succeed, which underlies the virtue of *perseverance.* Finding common cause with the spirit of our surroundings leads in the realm of social life to *faithfulness* and a fruitful, ripe maturing of relationships.

JULY—CRAB

The Crab is connected with the enclosure of the rib-cage, the most complete inwardizing and rejection of the world, but also with the impulse to action. Actions which obliterate the outer world reach a culmination in *acts of murder.* The impulse to eliminate finds its proper place when it is not turned outwards but inwards towards one's own self, when it becomes *selflessness.* The killing out of all egoism, engendering in its place a warmth of life, leads to *purification.*

AUGUST – LION
If we turn back to the outer sense-world while the impulse of egoism still reigns, there is the danger of *thefts*. It is said that opportunity makes a thief, so that desires impel the will. The opposite is a heart filled out and surged through with sunny radiance and enthusiasm, which gives instead of takes. Such a heart is the source of *compassion*, equally stimulated by a situation around us. This desires nothing from the other but offers its help in *freedom*, while also ensuring the freedom of the other.

SEPTEMBER – VIRGIN
At the head of Christ's list stand *fornications*. This is inveighed against in the New Testament more than any other vice, yet it is probably too pedantic to assume that it was then so prevalent. The Virgin carries with her sheaf not only the maturity of the past but also the dissolving of form into chaos which makes way for the future cosmos. This future is not, however, to be gained by an assault of force based on egoism. If the virgin soul is to give birth to the higher nature of man it must be wooed by the creative spirit with the gentleness of chivalry and *courtesy*. This is more than mere politeness; it is the outer expression of inner respect for the other person, which forms the starting-point of any community, then as now. On this basis of respect we accept the other as he is, as phenomenon, and thus gain a feeling understanding of him or her. Courtesy becomes *tact of heart*.

This consonance between the 'evil thoughts' listed by Christ, the characteristics of the constellations, and the extended insight into the virtues given by Rudolf Steiner, can together be an incentive to live with the latter throughout the year.[4]

Appendix 5
A Manichaean Hymn to Jesus

We stand all of one mind
And we will reach out our hands in invocation,
And rest our eyes upon Thy form.
And our mouths will we open to invoke Thee
And our tongues prepare for praise.
Thee we invoke, who art fullness of life.
Thee we praise, Jesus the Brilliant! New Aeon!
Thou art, Thou art the God who performs Truth,
A noble Healer, the most beloved Son, the most loved Ego.

Come with grace, liberated Lord!
Come with aid, good Spirit, Apostle with peace!
Helper of the frail and Conqueror of the aggressors!
Come with grace, new Lord!
Come with grace, Redeemer of the subjected, Healer of the wounded!
Come with grace, Awakener of the sleeping and Arouser of the sleepy, Thou who causest the dead to arise!
Come with grace, mighty God and hallowing Voice!
Come with grace, true Word, great Luminary, and flooding Light!
Come with grace, new Lord and new Day!
Come with grace, Gift of the good, Blessing of the frail, Revered of the holy!
Come with grace, loving Father and just Judge of those who have sought refuge with thee!
Come with grace, Father, Thou who art our stout protection and firm faith! . . .

Now, Just Dealer, peace be upon us!
And have mercy upon us and love us, Benefactor who art all love!

And reckon us not together with the troublemakers (?)!
Save those who have sought refuge and have mercy upon us!
O Most Beloved and Loving!

We have beheld Thee, New Aeon,
And we have fallen at thy feet, Thou who art all love.
Drunk with joy we have seen Thee, loving Lord.
And we avow Thy name, Messiah.
Sunder us from amid the sinful,
And free us from amid the aggressors!
O Lord, we are Thine own, have mercy upon us!
Hasten hither and subdue the sinners!
For they are become insolent and have spoken thus:
'We are the ones. And there is none like us.'
Therefore exercise Thy power, and cast the aggressors and enemies (?) down...

We praise Thy name, that is all Light,
And Thy noble greatness, that is all Freedom.
Praise be to Thy name, Father!
And devotion to Thy greatness!
So be it, now and ever more!

From G. Widengren, trans. C. Kessler,
Mani and Manichaeism

Notes

All references are to the work of Rudolf Steiner unless otherwise stated. Published English translations are available via Rudolf Steiner Press, London, and Anthroposophic Press, New York. Out of print titles and typescripts are available from Rudolf Steiner House Library, London.

GA = Gesamtausgabe, Steiner's collected works in the original German.

Introduction (pages 1–3)

1. *An Esoteric Cosmology,* lecture 2, 26 May 1906.
2. Ibid.

1. Mani's Life and Personality (pages 5–11)

1. *The Temple Legend,* lecture 6, 11 November 1904.
2. *The Gospel of St John* (Hamburg), lecture 1, 25 May 1908.
3. G. Widengren, see Preface.

2. The Cosmic Drama (pages 13–16)

1. Abridged from report by S.N.C. Lieu (see Preface) of al Nadin, The Fihrist, Baghdad 988, trans. B. Dodge, New York 1970.

3. Stages of Evolution (pages 17–22)

1. *The Gospel of St Matthew,* lecture 2, 2 September 1910. *The Apocalypse of St John,* lecture 2, 19 June 1908.
2. *The East in the Light of the West,* lecture 9, 31 August 1909.
3. *Christ and the Spiritual World,* lecture 1, 28 December 1913.
4. *The Spiritual Hierarchies and the Physical World,* lecture 9, 18 April 1909 (i).
5. *Man in the Light of Occultism, Theosophy and Philosophy,* lecture 3, 5 June 1912.
6. *Manifestations of Karma,* lecture 10, 27 May 1910.

4. Redemption (pages 23–27)

1. S.N.C. Lieu, *Manichaeism in Mesopotamia and the Roman East*, Leiden NL 1994.
2. *Festivals of the Seasons*, 26 December 1914.
3. Quoted by S.N.C. Lieu, see Preface.
4. *The Effects of Occult Development*, lecture 6, 25 March 1913.
5. *Building Stones for an Understanding of the Mystery of Golgotha*, lecture 7, 19 April 1917.
   The Redemption of Thinking, lecture 1, 22 May 1920.
   Lecture of 15 May 1921 in *Anthroposophy*, Vol. 8, No 2.
6. *The Temple Legend, passim*, lectures given during November 1904.
7. *The Spiritual Guidance of Mankind*, lecture 2, 7 June 1911.

5. Twelve Realms of Light (pages 29–34)

1. *An Esoteric Cosmology*, lecture 2, 26 May 1906.
2. *Egyptian Myths and Mysteries*, lecture 6, 8 September 1908.
3. Hugo Reimann, *Manichaeismus, das Christentum der Freiheit*, Dornach CH 1980.
4. *The Effects of Spiritual Development*, lecture 7, 26 March 1913.
5. *The East in the Light of the West*, lecture 9, 31 August 1909.
6. *The Temple Legend*, lecture 6, 11 November 1904.
7. *Guidance in Esoteric Training*, From the Contents of the Esoteric School.
8. *At the Gates of Spiritual Science*, lecture 4, 25 August 1906.
9. *From Symptom to Reality in Modern History*, lecture 5, 26 October 1918.

6. Fivefold Aspects (pages 35–40)

1. *Christ and the Spiritual World*, lecture 4, 31 December 1913.
2. *World History and the Mysteries in the Light of Anthroposophy*, lecture 4, 27 December 1923.
3. *The Wrong and Right Use of Esoteric Knowledge*, lecture 3, 25 November 1917.
4. Hugo Reimann, see chapter 5, note 3.
5. *The World of the Senses and World of the Spirit*, lecture 1, 27 December 1911; see also lecture 4, of 30 December.

7. Manichaean Community (pages 41–47)

1. *Occult History,* lecture 4, 30 December 1910.
2. *The Redemption of Thinking,* lecture 1, 25 May 1920.
3. Albert Steffen, *Mani,* Dornach CH. Not translated.

8. The Expansion and Contraction of Manichaeism (pages 49–53)

1. *Building Stones for an Understanding of the Mystery of Golgotha,* lecture 7, 19 April 1917.
2. Lecture of 15 May 1921, in *Anthroposophy,* Vol. 8, No. 2.
3. *Festivals of the Seasons,* 26 December 1914.
   The Redemption of Thinking, lecture 1, 22 May 1920.
4. Hugo Reimann, see chapter 5, note 3.
5. *Karmic Relationships,* Vol. III, lecture 5, 11 July 1924.
6. *The Temple Legend,* lecture 6, 11 November 1904.
7. See Note 1.
8. Albert Steffen, *Epoche,* Dornach CH 1944.

9. Mani's Individuality (pages 55–58)

1. *Bhagavad Gita,* lecture 3, 30 December 1912.
2. 'On the Awakenings in the Gospels' Undated Typescript K1.
3. *The Temple Legend,* lecture 6, 11 November 1904.
4. See Note 2.
   Christmas, lecture 6, 30 December 1904.
5. See Note 2.
   The Gospel of St Luke, lecture 10, 24 September 1909.
6. See Notes 2 and 3.
7. *The East in the Light of the West,* lecture 9, 31 August 1909.
8. The Mission of Folk Souls, lecture 7, 12 June 1910 (ii).
9. See Note 3.
10. See Note 2.
11. *Mysteries of the East and of Christianity,* lecture 4, 7 February 1913.
12. *Zur Geschichte und aus den Inhalten ... der esoterischen Schule,* GA 264, p. 239.
13. *Correspondence and Documents,* the 'Barr Document', 1907.
14. Lecture of 27 September 1911, in *Anthroposophical Quarterly,* Vol. 5, No. 4.
15. See Note 12, p. 240.

10. The Future Role of Manichaeans (pages 59–63)

1. *An Esoteric Cosmology,* lecture 2, 26 May 1906.
2. Lecture of 15 January 1914, in *Anthroposophical News Sheet* 1946, p. 363 (NSL 346).
3. *Aspects of Human Evolution,* lecture 5, 3 July 1917.
4. Lecture of 7 November 1915, in *Anthroposophical News Sheet,* 1940 p. 19 (R 74).
5. *The Ego,* lecture 1, 4 December 1909.
6. *The Temple Legend,* lecture 6, 11 November 1904.
7. *Festivals of the Seasons,* lectures of 26 December 1914.
8. *Planetary Spheres and their Influence,* lecture 6, 19 November 22.
9. *The Apocalypse of St John,* lecture 8, 25 June 1908.
10. *Correspondence and Documents,* the 'Barr Document', 1907.
11. See Note 6.
12. *At the Gates of Spiritual Science,* lecture 8, 29 August 1906.
13. See Note 6.
14. *The Apocalypse of St John,* lecture 12, 30 June 1908.
15. *Occult Movements in the Nineteenth Century,* lecture 5, 18 October 1915.
16. *Fundamentals of Esotericism,* lecture 13, 8 October 1905.

Conclusion (pages 65–66)

1. *The Apocalypse of St John,* lecture 11, 29 June 1908.
2. *The East in the Light of the West,* lecture 9, 31 August 1909.
3. *The Apocalypse of St John,* lecture 6, 23 June 1908.
4. *The Challenge of the Times,* lecture 5, 7 December 1918.

Appendix 1. A Note on Mithraism (pages 67–68)

1. *Building Stones for an Understanding of the Mystery of Golgotha,* lecture 8, 24 April 1917.

Appendix 4. Cosmic Forces of Vice and Virtue (pages 77–81)

1. See Chapter 5, Note 7.
2. *Man in the Light of Occultism, Theosophy and Philosophy,* lecture 6, 8 June 1912.
3. *Eurythmy as Visible Speech,* lecture 10, 7 July 1924.
4. See also H. Witzenmann , trans. D. Aldan, *The Virtues, a Series of Contemplations,* New York 1975.